Israel,
My Chosen People

Other Kanaan Publications:

A FORETASTE OF HEAVEN (Autobiography)
BUILDING A WALL OF PRAYER
FATHER OF COMFORT
I WILL GIVE YOU THE TREASURES OF DARKNESS
MORE PRECIOUS THAN GOLD
MY ALL FOR HIM
NATURE OUT OF CONTROL?
REPENTANCE — THE JOY-FILLED LIFE
STRONG IN THE TIME OF TESTING
THE HIDDEN TREASURE IN SUFFERING
TURNING DEFEAT INTO VICTORY
YOURS IS THE VICTORY AND MAJESTY

Available in Australia from:
> Evangelical Sisterhood of Mary
> P.O.Box 781, Camden NSW 2570

Available in the British Isles from:
> Evangelical Sisterhood of Mary
> Radlett, Herts WD7 8DE

Available in Canada from:
> Evangelical Sisterhood of Mary
> 4285 Heritage Drive, Tracy, NB, E5L 1B2
and: R.R.1, Millet, AB, T0C 1Z0

Available in Germany from:
> Evangelical Sisterhood of Mary
> P.O.Box 13 01 29, D-64241 Darmstadt

Available in the USA from:
> Evangelical Sisterhood of Mary
> P.O.Box 30022, Phoenix, AZ 85046-0022

Internet: http://www.kanaan.org

Israel,
My Chosen People

M. Basilea Schlink

KANAAN PUBLICATIONS
Evangelical Sisterhood of Mary
Darmstadt, Germany and Radlett, England

Designed and produced in England for Kanaan Publications by
Gazelle Creative Productions Ltd, Concorde House, Grenville Place
Mill Hill, London NW7 3SA

Contents

About the Author

Mother Basilea (Dr. Klara Schlink) was born in Darmstadt, Germany, in 1904. She grew up in Brunswick, where for many years her father was head of the Technical University. Despite an intellectually and culturally stimulating homelife, she was inwardly searching, and not until she met Jesus as her Saviour at the age of seventeen did she find what she was looking for. She trained as a kindergarten teacher and social worker, attended Bible college and went on to study history of art, philosophy, theology and psychology, receiving her doctorate at the University of Hamburg in 1934. A registered member of the Confessing Church, she became National President of the Women's Division of the German Student Christian Movement. During World War II she served as travelling lecturer for a missionary society in Germany.

In Darmstadt, in 1947, together with her co-worker Erika Madauss (now Mother Martyria), she founded the Evangelical Sisterhood of Mary within the framework of the German Evangelical [Protestant] Church. From its small beginnings the sisterhood has grown into an international, inter-denominational organization with branches in various parts of the world and its headquarters at the little land of Canaan (Kanaan), Darmstadt. In 1967 the Canaan Franciscan Brotherhood was established.

Mother Basilea Schlink is the author of more than 100 titles, with translations in over 60 languages, and has appeared in films and videos produced at Kanaan and televised in widely differing places such as North America, the Middle East, Scandinavia, East Asia and Australia.

Her personal encounter with Israel is described more fully in a chapter of her autobiography (first published in English in 1975), from which excerpts have been included at the back of this book.

Foreword

A visitor entering our Mother House Chapel in Darmstadt may be surprised to find a menorah, a seven-branched candelabra, opposite the lectern. An unexpected sight in a small German chapel. But for our sisterhood it has a special significance. The gift of Danes, who as a people so bravely supported the Jewish cause during World War II, it is a constant reminder of our national guilt and a summons to pray for Israel. Over the years we have been joined by many friends from home and abroad on Friday evenings, the Sabbath Eve, for a service of repentance and intercession for Israel, which culminates in the Sabbath candles being lit at the menorah. This kindling of the Sabbath candles is a symbolic act, for each new Sabbath brings us closer to the day when God's chosen people will be a blessing for all nations (Zechariah 8).

The awareness of Israel's unique role in God's eternal purposes has always been alive in Mother Basilea. After Hitler's rise to power, in 1933, pressure was exerted on her while National President of the Women's Division of the German Student Christian Movement to accept the Aryan paragraph, which would bar Jewish Christians from the movement. She refused to comply, persuading the group to reject the demand.

From 1939 to 1944, in her function as travelling lecturer, she risked her life and career during this politically sinister period by speaking publicly of her convictions. Though informers were frequently present at the lectures she held throughout Germany, she felt constrained to speak of the election of the Jews and their leading position and commission to all nations in the millennium kingdom. Summoned before the Gestapo, she was interrogated for hours, though, inexplicably, only because of her challenge to follow Jesus; in their opinion there was only 'one true Führer'.

At the end of the war, clearly perceiving God's hand of judgment in the destruction of many German towns, including her hometown Darmstadt, she was used by the Lord to start a movement of repentance, which was to have nationwide repercussions. Repentance was the keynote of the revival among the Girls' Bible Study Groups, which gave rise to our Evangelical Sisterhood of Mary, and it was repentance that gave birth to a deep love for Israel in our fellowship.

The message of repentance for our national crime against the Jews made a decisive impact on the Christian conscience in Germany, greatly changing the attitude towards the Jews, as leading clergymen have attested.

Tragically, anti-Semitism is not just a thing of the past: hatred of the Jews is flaring up anew in Germany and other parts of the world. In the not-too-distant future we may all be challenged about our relationship to Israel, and ultimately to God. Will history repeat itself? Will we Christians once more be guilty of silence and passiveness?

It is with such thoughts in mind that we should read this book, which in many ways is a historical document, written in 1958 while Israel was a young state, her land and capital city divided by barbed wire, and the population half its present size. Inwardly and outwardly Israel has changed considerably since then and, sadly enough, the detrimental influence of our Western nations is also leaving its mark there. Yet it should not surprise us that the greatest struggle between light and darkness should occur in God's land. Does this not stir us all the more to prayer? As Mother Basilea writes in one of her pamphlets, 'Israel needs our help now...God is waiting for praying people, who first humble themselves before God because of their own sins and then because of the sins of their people — and this goes especially for us Germans in view of our national crime towards Israel...He is waiting for praying people, who will battle in faith for Israel...' (*A Cry from the Heart for Israel*, August 1984).

Whoever loves Jesus will love the people He loves. What the Word of God says about Israel will not fail to come to pass: 'Blessed be every one who blesses you, and cursed be every one who curses you' (Numbers 24:9).

Because of the prophetic nature of this book and its startling relevance for today, many requests have come for its republication with the result that this new English translation has been made of the original German edition.

The Sisters of Mary

Darmstadt, Germany, March 1987

11

PART ONE

The Time of Israel's Affliction:
The Time of Our People's Guilt

Chapter 1

The Great Crime
Against the Chosen People,
Born of Hatred of God

BEFORE OUR EYES there passes an almost endless procession of thousands upon thousands of human beings, old and young alike, men, women and children. Day after day and night after night, from 1942 to 1945, the freight trains rolled on steadily with their human cargo. Herded together like cattle in unbelievable conditions, these pitiful victims were being transported to extermination camps like Auschwitz, Treblinka, Maidanek, Belzec, Gross-Rosen and Sobibor. When this human load was discharged, it was not dealt with even as cattle would have been. No, what took place would have been shameful even in the treatment of animals. Authentic reports reveal:

> In the hot summer months as many as forty dead would be found in a single cattle car. When the few survivors were unloaded, they were so overcome with thirst that they threw themselves like animals into the muddy puddles beside the railway track...
>
> Then columns began to form and were marched to the first crematoria where they stood

in queues, as though waiting outside a food-store in time of famine or for the theatres to open on a first night. Hardly an hour later flames would begin to shoot skywards...Five giant ovens blazed day and night in Auschwitz [and similarly in other death camps], and whenever they were on the point of dying down, more human beings would be brought to replenish these blazing furnaces of wood and human flesh. The stars paled in their livid glow. The air was poisoned by the sickly smell of singeing hair and burning corpses...

Nearby were fires in the open where children's bodies were flung, the living as well as the dead. One could hear their screams and see the flames playing round their tender bodies. (Cf. Lucie Adelsberger, *Auschwitz.*)

In addition to the millions who were murdered in the gas chambers and in the mobile substitutes converted from vans, and burnt in the crematoria, there were further millions who died in the concentration camps from starvation and by execution, through epidemics and illness, in each case aggravated by the appalling treatment they received. As the end of the war drew near the ovens burnt still more furiously, fed with human bodies which they consumed relentlessly day and night.

How could such things happen? How could such fiendish horrors, which have been given only the briefest mention here, take place in the twentieth century — in the so-called age of human progress?

There was definitely something satanic behind it: a passionate rebellion against God Himself for having given us a conscience and for making us accountable to Him as Judge. Only the mind of a person possessed by hatred could say, as Hitler said to Rauschning, 'Conscience is a Jewish invention!' and, 'There is no room for two chosen peoples!'

This one mind, consumed with hatred and finding fuel in many other hearts and minds, spread hatred among our people to fearful effect. It was hatred against God, because it was to the Jewish people that God had revealed Himself through His holy Ten Commandments, through His prophets, through Jesus and His apostles, thus appealing to the consciences of all human beings. It was a diabolical hatred, in reality directed not against a particular race but against God Himself. (A purely racial issue could never have generated such an intensity of hatred.) Behind it all was envy — diabolical envy — because the Jewish people, and not the Nordic race, bore the mark of divine election and had been chosen for a world mission. God was justified in the choice of His people; for the Nordic race, which considered itself more noble and of greater purity than any other, has in fact proved itself to be baser, more despicable and more inhuman than the most primitive tribe on the face of the earth.

On the other hand, the 'loathsome' Jew, characterized as being 'subhuman', 'brutal' and 'murderous', has proved, in the midst of the most inhuman suffering, to be truly heroic, noble and great, despite the natural weaknesses that the Jews share with every other people because of the Fall. Their heroism is revealed in all objective reports on the concentration and death camps, and particularly in the account of the Warsaw Ghetto uprising. There is no deception in suffering. It shows what a person's true values are.

In this terrible persecution and extermination of the Jews the ultimate motive behind anti-Semitism becomes evident, and hatred of the Jews can be seen for what it really is. Every Jew, by his very existence, points towards God, towards the election and calling of Abraham, towards the election of Israel as a people for God's own possession, singled out from among all other nations, particularly loved by God, who gave them special graces and promises and who kept them from perishing throughout their thousands of years of history. Every Jew is a reminder that God is the holy God, the God of the Ten Commandments. Every Jew is a reminder that God lives, that He pronounces blessings and curses and fulfils them both.

The Jew and his destiny are a living proof of the existence of God, as even a rationalist like Frederick the Great was forced to acknowledge. Once challenged by the king to provide proof of the existence of God, the pious statesman Ziethen replied, 'Your Majesty, the Jews!' at which Frederick the Great fell silent.

Chapter 2

Why Anti-Semitism
Is Not Justified

IF A CAREFUL EXAMINATION is made of the accusations that allegedly justify the hatred and ostracism of the Jews, they are found to be without much substance.

It is claimed that by nature they are profiteers, second-hand dealers and extortioners. But if this assertion is considered more carefully in the light of their history, it becomes evident that, as a people, the Jews have proved to be honourable, noble and capable in whatever their profession, as is convincingly shown today in the state of Israel. It is never admitted that it was we, the Gentiles, who excluded the Jews since the early Middle Ages (the eleventh and twelfth centuries) from the guilds, from the body of respectable merchants, from the ranks of craftsmen and farmers; that it was we who barred them from the learned professions, leaving them only the less honourable occupations, for which we considered ourselves to be too refined. It was we who compelled them to be money-lenders and second-hand dealers and who shut them up like prisoners in ghettos.

All that, however, was never mentioned when it came to loading them with insults. It was we, the 'Christian nations', who deprived the Jews of their rights and then with brazen impudence impressed on our children throughout the centuries the 'irreversible fact': 'The Jew is good for nothing; he is both too lazy and incompetent to carry on a trade or farming; he is capable only of amassing wealth by shady business deals and swindling.' How painful for the Jews to be branded with these calumnies!

In the mid eighteen hundreds, after centuries of being subjected to restrictive regulations, confined to ghettos and treated as outcasts, the Jews saw the doors to various professions open to them. It soon became evident how capable a people they are. Among them appeared first-rate doctors, scholars and scientists, lawyers, industrialists and leading merchants.

What was the result? They were envied and insulted because of their competence and intellectual ability, which enabled them to rise to the top of every profession. Yet here in Germany, for instance, their earnings, through taxation, were used to benefit the nation. Moreover, as is well known, many Jews were active on a large scale as benefactors to the poor, frequently supporting social and Christian organizations and, in sacrificial humaneness, bringing aid as doctors and volunteer workers to many in need. It was, therefore, with good reason that before 1933 many streets and public places in Germany were named after Jews.

Like every other German, the Jews fought for the German fatherland. Their bravery and fighting capacity on the front was revealed by the high percentage of Jews awarded decorations.

Why was there no resentment when Austrians or Hungarians or members of other peoples, who had settled among us, proved their abilities, made their fortunes and won public esteem? Why was it always against the Jews that this hostile attitude was adopted?

In medieval Europe they were persecuted and massacred on a number of occasions. From the latter half of the sixteenth century onwards they were confined to ghettos. Even after the dawn of the Age of Enlightenment their influence in positions of authority was resented and many were glad whenever Jews were degraded and relegated to inferior posts. And in more recent times it came to the point where they were held in the utmost contempt and subjected to unimaginable cruelty.

Having always desired to justify such hostility, their foes did not scruple to fabricate incriminating evidence. If something went wrong in government affairs or during a war, the blame attached to some group or class or state was shifted to the Jews and a persecution was started against them. Already in medieval times the Jews were made the scapegoat for the Black Death: they were said to have poisoned the wells. In every age there have been new evils for which they have been held responsible.

The climax of unbelievable lies and appalling cruelties was reached in Germany between the years 1933 and 1945. None of us can disclaim moral responsibility for this inhuman crime which has taken place among our people. In so far as we condoned the rejection and condemnation of the Jews we are all enmeshed in the net of the anti-Semitic lie which instigated the crime. We are to blame if we left unchallenged those statements calculated to stir up hatred: 'They are profiteers at the expense of our people.' — 'They are contaminating the intellectual and spiritual powers of our people.' We heaped guilt upon ourselves if we listened to lies and accepted without contradiction references to the Jews as the root of all our ills. Yes, all of us are guilty in some way of having fallen victim to what must be termed the 'anti-Semitic psychosis'.

According to statistics, it is not true that there was a larger percentage of Jews with a criminal record or a greater number of their people, than of any other nationality, in prison or penitentiary. As a general rule it is unfavourable social conditions that are most likely to breed anti-social behaviour and it is individuals from such backgrounds who fill the prisons and penitentiaries. Yet, strikingly, this is not the case with the Jews, who, until their emancipation began in the early nineteenth century, were treated as outcasts.

If, however, a Jew happened to cheat someone or commit some offence, this was given undue publicity and used as a pretext to condemn all Jews and possibly even to instigate a pogrom against them. Conversely, a criminal offence committed by a person of any other nationality was considered to be something involving only himself and not the whole of his people.

How utterly false all of these excuses for anti-Semitism are, has now become evident in the new state of Israel. Here God gives the lie to the derogatory assertions and slanderous statements that have been fabricated or passed on without examination, charges such as 'the Jews are nothing but work-shy profiteers'. Now the whole world can see that the Jewish people in their own land successfully practise not only all trades as well as farming, but even undertake pioneer work in the most adverse conditions of desert and swamp, making truly remarkable achievements. They are mastering the greatest difficulties and transforming what was, for almost two thousand years, barren land into a blossoming garden.

Yes, this state of 'good-for-nothing' Jews absorbed a mass immigration, which more than doubled the population in the first three-and-a-half years of the state's existence. This is in contrast with prosperous, long-existing and economically stable countries like Canada and Australia, which in ten years increased only by one-quarter of their existing population. Furthermore, whereas only the young, the strong, and the skilled were permitted to settle in Canada and Australia, the great majority of the immigrants coming to Israel had barely escaped with their lives from the terrors of persecution; and among them were many who were old and sick. These were people who had endured the severest physical and mental trials.

The slander that the Jews are cowards and poor soldiers has clearly been refuted in Israel. In 1948 the infant Jewish state, numbering about 650,000

Jewish inhabitants, was surrounded by 40,000,000
Arabs. But although they were opposed by the
combined armies of seven Arab states, profes-
sionally trained, partly drilled and led by British
officers, they emerged victorious.

This victory confirmed the proclamation of the
state of Israel as having inaugurated a new phase
in redemptive history. God is bringing to a close
the period of judgment and chastening for His
people, which has lasted almost two thousand
years. God has led them out of the dispersion back
into their homeland, the land of their fathers, to
demonstrate there to all the world what they are
made of — their abilities, their characteristics and
the principles of their conduct. There are ne'er-do-
wells among all nationalities and they exist among
the Jewish people too. But in the state of Israel it
can now be seen that here is a people who endeav-
our to keep the Ten Commandments and thus take
the living God seriously, honouring His name.
Often this cannot be said in equal measure of
Christian countries.

The fourth commandment, for example, is still
kept sacred. On the Sabbath life comes to a virtual
standstill. How impressive is the beginning of the
Sabbath in Jerusalem, which I experienced on one
of my journeys! The Sabbath horn sounds through
the streets, and in a moment a large, busy city is
reduced to silence. It is as if at sunset, with the
sound of the Sabbath horn, the city becomes
shrouded in a silence like that of eternity. There
is hardly a car to be seen; the few that remain are
driven mostly by Christians and Moslems. One

witnesses here an entire people — even if many may conform only outwardly — abiding by God's commandments and honouring as a nation this commandment to keep holy the Sabbath Day. Even the cinema, a power that holds so many in thrall today, must surrender its claims on the Sabbath Eve and close its doors.

Also in scientific, political and cultural events God is repeatedly given the glory. Some time ago the foundation stone was laid for the new planetarium in Jerusalem. On this foundation stone were engraved the words of Psalm 148: 'Praise the Lord, sun and moon, praise him, all you shining stars!' In contrast, we hear that in the weighty addresses given by distinguished Christian statesmen and scholars on the occasion of the geophysical year, 1957, the name of God was not mentioned even once.

Israel's devout attitude is also shown in President Ben-Zvi's speech at the ninth anniversary of the foundation of the state. He said, 'Thanks to the "Rock of Israel" the Israel Defence Forces have succeeded in driving back the enemy.' In this Jewish state glory is given to God, the 'Rock of Israel', though human effort undoubtedly plays a great role in the present development of the land of Israel.

The Prime Minister, David Ben-Gurion, is constantly occupied with one book which he knows by heart, to which he continually refers, which to him is law and moral support and which, as he says, makes everything clear to him: Nasser, the oil question, the military superiority of Israel over her neighbours and the absolute assurance of final victory — and this book is the Bible. So writes a Swiss journalist after a conversation with David Ben-Gurion (*Weltwoche*, Zurich, January 18, 1957).

Yes, Holy Scripture is a living force among this people, and its influence can be felt in Israel's public life. Where else other than in Israel are the returning harvest wagons decorated with ribbons bearing Scripture texts? Where else are harvest festivals celebrated with dancing to the accompaniment of Psalm-singing? Where else are the premises of national exhibitions hung with Scripture posters? In what other country does a Bible competition form the highlight of a jubilee, as it did in the tenth anniversary celebrations of the foundation of the state of Israel? So widespread was the interest shown in the contest that cafés and cinemas were deserted while people gathered round their radios at home to follow each stage of the contest, eager to know who was most versed in the Scriptures. It has now become evident in Israel that the Jews are not a godless, degenerate people, but rather a people whom God has chosen for Himself, and among whom He wants to make Himself known in everyday life. Although many are drifting away from the faith of their fathers, a God-fearing attitude still prevails. Their precious heritage, which stems from God and His Word, is an undeniable reality, and the hour has arrived when it will come to life again.

Chapter 3

Christianity's Share in Hatred of the Jews

THAT THE IMAGE of the Jews as a godless, sub-versive, immoral people has proved to be completely false shows that behind this hatred there must be deeper reasons than are generally put forward. All arguments in support of anti-Semitism are shallow and irrelevant. The real target of this hatred is the election of this people and thus the One who elected them: God. According to Holy Scripture, this will become particularly evident in the end times, which are characterized by hatred against God. Then the persecution against the Jews — and for that matter against the Christians too — will reach its climax.

Seeing that this diabolical hatred is directed against Jews and Christians alike, is it not all the more shocking to find that hatred of the Jews did not originate solely in the world of the godless and the God-haters, but that this hatred, and thus the terrible crime of this century against the Jews, also has its roots in the history of Christianity?

In the Early Church, Jews and Gentiles were gathered round Jesus as one body, the dividing wall between Jew and Gentile having been broken down. They were one flock with one Shepherd. Later on, the situation changed. More Gentiles entered the Christian community so that the ratio of Gentiles to Jews steadily grew. Then, by and by, the Jews who had not yet entered the Christian fold, were regarded no longer as brothers in the belief in the one revealed God, but as aliens, even enemies. In spite of all the difficulties and struggles that arose, there would have been every reason to have been humbly and lovingly disposed towards them, considering that it was from them that we have received the law and the prophets and the Lord Jesus. It is not without reason that the Apostle Paul exhorts us who believe in Christ not to adopt a superior attitude towards the Jews but to remain humbly aware that the Jews are the root of the tree. They bear us, not we them, for we are only grafted in (Romans 11). But the evil one succeeded in luring the Christian Church away from this humble, brotherly attitude when, in self-glory, she appropriated all the graces and promises meant for Israel, thereby expunging Israel from God's redemptive history.

Such arrogance made it possible for those assertions promoting hatred of the Jews to thrive even within Christendom. It was argued, 'Did not God Himself say in His Word that the Jews are a stubborn, disobedient people, full of sins, lies and unfaithfulness?' Admittedly, the Holy Scriptures speak thus of the people of Israel; there is no denying that. But what verdict would the Lord pronounce upon the Christian Church today? And what would He say to all those Christians who in the name of the Crucified One caused such a bloodbath among the Jews in the Holy Land as well as here in this country at the time of the Crusades? What blindness then but even more so today to condemn others when we ourselves are steeped far more grievously in sin! He who is of the truth sees his own sin, casts no stone at another Christian denomination or at his elder brother Israel, but judges himself instead. And this is precisely what Israel does. So writes Lilli Simon of the Jews and their attitude towards their sins or, more specifically, their national sins, in *Stimme der Gemeinde* (September 1, 1957, p. 522), under the heading, 'Israel und die Araber':

> Surely the Old Testament with its historical books is a striking example. Whether Joshua holds a national address for the people; whether Samuel gives a synopsis of their history; whether Solomon dedicates the temple; whether Ezra exhorts and reforms the people returning from long captivity; these self-portrayals and surveys of their own past are always public confessions of guilt before God. Written history of Israel has always been self-accusation. Such an attitude of self-criticism and self-accusation, repentance and confession of guilt for what they have done and for what has happened — very uncommon among Western peoples — also characterizes life in modern Israel. Only when seeing eye to eye with God can a person or nation acquire such an attitude.

Furthermore, in considering the malicious charge that even the Word of God presents Israel as disobedient and stubborn, we are to remember that Israel is God's first-born son. Whereas a father tends to overlook the faults of another man's child, he takes his son to task and disciplines him, being especially strict in dealing with his first-born as a warning to the others. This we can see from God's disciplinary measures with Israel, which are meant to serve as a deterrent example for us. For all the nations Israel has been set as a sign that God hates and punishes sin.

> I will pursue them with war, starvation, and disease, and all the nations of the world will be horrified at what they see.   Jeremiah 29:18 GNB

From this are we to conclude that judgment applies to Israel alone? No, the Lord says,

> I have begun to punish my own people, so should you go free? No, you shall not evade punishment. I will call for war against all the peoples of the earth.   Jeremiah 25:29 LB

So it is not because Israel is particularly sinful that severe divine judgments have come upon her, but because she is the chosen people of God and the Scriptures say, 'The Lord reproves him whom he loves, as a father the son in whom he delights' (Proverbs 3:12; cf. Hebrews 12:6).

How, then, did we arrive at such a distorted and unscriptural conclusion about God's dealings with the Jews? Our arrogance has made us blind and incapable of forming an opinion in love. This is the difference between the way God the Father looks upon His people Israel and the way we Christians have looked upon His first-born. God regards His people with fatherly love. In the midst of judgment He pauses to say,

> Is not Ephraim my dear son, the child in whom I delight? Though I often speak against him, I still remember him. Therefore my heart yearns for him; I have great compassion for him.
>
> Jeremiah 31:20 NIV

If only we Christians had looked upon Israel with the same kindness! Did not our Lord and Master call us above all to love? But instead of looking upon Israel with eyes of love, we looked, and still look, upon her with censuring arrogance. It is hardly surprising that such a condemning attitude led us to pass an unfavourable judgment upon her. For is not Israel a people full of weaknesses, flaws and sins, as we and other peoples are?

If we had looked upon Israel with eyes of love, we would have taken to heart her struggles and sufferings in the past, recalling the immensely difficult paths she had to tread through the desert. We would have asked ourselves whether we, as Christians, would have been capable of passing through such severe trials of faith as the people of Israel had to undergo. Israel, doomed to destruction, had to approach the Red Sea before the miracle happened. They had to wander, old people and children included, through the cruel wilderness under the glare of the burning desert sun, with nothing to eat or drink, facing ruin — a whole people on the brink of death.

Who of us would have been so strong in faith, firmly believing in a miracle of God? Who would not have been full of anxiety and trepidation and have rebelled at so hard a lot? Who of us would have had the courage to set out for Canaan, the Promised Land, which was reported to be inhabited by a people of great stature, even giants, living in fortified cities? Israel, it must be remembered, was an unarmed shepherd-people journeying through the wilderness with young and old in her midst. Considering that we often fail to trust in God's help even in the little difficulties and vexations of everyday life, how can we throw stones at the allegedly cowardly, disobedient and stiff-necked people of Israel? We do so because we are blind to the sin in our own hearts, and because we have never really taken the Word of God seriously.

We talk so much about a veil covering the eyes of Israel. Certainly, a veil exists until the Jews recognize their Messiah, but is there not another veil hanging over our own eyes? Are we not often so blind that we read the clear words of Holy Scripture about Israel's election and yet fail to grasp their meaning and to act accordingly? Looked down upon by us for their spiritual blindness, often reviled as blasphemers, religious Jews have a reverence for the Word of God and His law and do not profane it. If we had stood in such holy awe of the Word of God, we would have paid heed to statements like the following:

> Those who strive against you [Israel] shall be as nothing and shall perish.   Isaiah 41:11

> He who touches you touches the apple of his eye.
> Zechariah 2:8

> Do not boast over the branches . . . Remember it is
> not you that support the root, but the root that
> supports you . . . So do not become proud, but
> stand in awe.   Romans 11:18,20

Whereas we show that we lack reverence for the
Word of God, it is an overwhelming experience to
see how the Jews, even the so-called non-religious
among them, stand in awe of it. On my travels
in Israel I have had innumerable encounters with
Jews who had emigrated from Germany, and I have
found that despite the inhuman treatment they had
received they do not return the violent hatred of
their tormentors. Again and again I was told, 'We
have been commanded not to hate but to love our
neighbour.' It could be that one day at God's throne
of judgment we Christians who have been trifling
with the Word of God shall be found guilty, whereas Israel will be acceptable to God because she
adhered to the truth she had recognized: the Ten
Commandments. We Christians have paid scant
regard to the ninth commandment and have slandered Israel. Furthermore, we have not taken seriously the fundamental law to love God and to
love our neighbour as ourselves. Our neighbour,
according to the interpretation of Jesus, is the one
who has fallen among the robbers. This description
perfectly matches that of Israel in the course of
history and especially nowadays. We have passed
by on the other side, thus sinning against the first
and greatest commandment of God: the commandment to love.

Indeed, we see the sins of others very well, but
we are blind to our own guilt. Down through the

centuries, right up to the present day, we accuse the Jews of having killed Jesus, whereas Jesus Himself prayed on the cross, 'Father, forgive them; for they know not what they do' (Luke 23:34). But what have we done? Quite apart from the fact that we are also to blame for the crucifixion of Jesus (Scripture clearly states that both Jews and Gentiles put Jesus to death — see Matthew 20:18f.), we have added to His sufferings by afflicting the Jews. In all the cruel persecutions perpetrated against the chosen people, from whom Jesus came and who are His special love, we have despised Jesus. What we do to the people of God, we do to God Himself, as His Word says: 'In all their affliction he was afflicted' (Isaiah 63:9).

Woe betide us when we are called to account! Then it may turn out that Jesus finds His likeness in Israel and not in us. Two-and-a-half thousand years of immeasurable suffering have made her poor and wretched, so that she does indeed resemble the image of Jesus, 'despised and rejected by men'. But we who confess Jesus with our lips may one day be far away from Him, because we were unwilling to suffer contempt, misery, rejection, hatred and torment. Apart from those who have suffered martyrdom in one form or another, the Christian Church as a whole, since Constantine, has enjoyed esteem and, seated upon her throne, she has looked down from this exalted position in judgment upon her elder brother. It may not be mere chance that the unbiased viewer of the statues 'Synagogue' and 'Ecclesia' at the southern portal of Strasbourg Cathedral involuntarily finds his sympathy directed to 'Synagogue', which depicts brokenness and humility, rather than to 'Ecclesia', radiating pride and arrogance.

Because we Christians have generally adopted towards the Jews a loveless, arrogant and critical attitude, foreign to the spirit of Jesus, hatred of the Jews could gain such momentum over the centuries in Christian countries, such as our own country Germany, finally erupting in the events of the most recent past. The dreadful avalanche that has now descended to the shame and dishonour of the German people gathered force slowly through the centuries. At first it all seemed harmless. In the realm of theological discourse doubt was expressed about the Jews still being the people of the covenant. Had not the Christians taken their place as the people of the new covenant? All the negative statements of Scripture were utilized to this end.

In the beginning anti-Judaism was mainly confined to the clergy, whose theological dissertations were conducted not only without love but very often in open malice. To justify their stance, they argued that the Jews had killed Jesus and had persistently refused to accept salvation. Yet in the background there often lurked very human fears of competition. In view of the clergy's attitude it was hardly surprising that soon the medieval Christian community was also seized with antagonism towards the Jews and that at the time of the Crusades, from the eleventh century onwards, the Jews were violently persecuted. Since the thirteenth century in England, France, Spain, Poland and Germany, extensive measures were adopted against them: expulsion, confinement to ghettos, deprivation of rights, and organized massacres — and this again and again in the name of Christian governments or segments of the population.

In this way the devil succeeded in making Christians prepare the ground for him. The stone that had started to roll became an avalanche because no one checked its descent. And so it grew in our times to a degree of bestial inhumanity far exceeding anything else the world had witnessed before. It was the wholesale slaughter of millions.

That hatred against the Jews, and the consequent attempt at their annihilation, reached such a peak in our times indicates that we are approaching the antichristian period, which is characterized by hatred of God and all who belong to Him. The hatred manifested by the forerunners of the Antichrist such as Hitler will reach its final climax in the antichristian era proper. Then those in Christendom who have supported anti-Semitism, will suddenly find themselves in the ranks of the Antichrist, whom they have unwittingly been serving. Perhaps they will not even recognize him as the Antichrist (just as many Christians in Germany failed to recognize Hitler as the enemy of God), but nonetheless they will incur the same judgment as the Antichrist.

At the close of the age there will be a new divide. Under the oppression of the Antichrist, Jews and true Christians will draw closer to each other. According to Daniel 12:1, the last days, the antichristian era, will be a time of unprecedented distress for the Jewish people, because the Anti-christ will war against all who fear God — Jews and, naturally, Christians too. The same may be inferred from the Book of Revelation. In Revelation 7, John describes the sealing of members of the Jewish tribes for the antichristian era.

As already stated, at the close of the age Jews and Christians will come under persecution from the Antichrist. As God's plan of salvation nears its final consummation after a period of two thousand years and hatred flares up against Him more than ever, there will be a bringing together of those who belong together because they fear the living God and give Him glory — Jews and Christians. A foreshadowing of this could be seen in the Nazi era when both Jews and Christians suffered persecution and were often found to-gether in concentration camps, although the Jews were by far the more fiercely persecuted. It is known, however, that Hitler intended to proceed with the same ruthlessness against the Christians after he had won the war. This bringing together of Jews and Christians, under common persecu-tion, will ripen into an even deeper union when the Messiah appears to the Jews.

Chapter 4

'The least of these my brethren' — What Have We Done to Them?

IN THE LAST DAYS many Christians will awaken. They will see what they have done — injured and persecuted the chosen people of God. Just as the Jews will break out in lamentation 'when they look on him whom they have pierced' and 'shall mourn for him, as one mourns for an only child, and weep bitterly over him, as one weeps over a first-born' (Zechariah 12:10), so will the Christians on their part be filled with grief and lamentation for having afflicted the people dear to God.

But then it will be too late to show them kindness. Now is the time for the New Testament people to awaken — now, before the last hour comes, and with it judgment. Today let us take our place at Jesus' side and look upon His people with His eyes, full of love and mercy. Then our hearts would ache to see this chosen people of God wandering through the centuries, wretched, despised, shunned, ostracized and afflicted with pain like the suffering Servant of God in Isaiah 53. Then, looking on them, we would be reminded of Him.

Israel, unintentionally and unwittingly, has become a spectacle before heaven and mankind, because she bears the features of the Servant of God. The sight of her should continually remind Christians of Jesus, despised, destitute, covered with bruises, afflicted, hated, persecuted, tormented, and hounded to death. Even if these marks borne by the people of God also indicate the chastening hand of God stretched out in judgment upon sinners, the fact remains that by these very dealings God proclaims Himself to be the Holy One of Israel.

We as Christians are to hold in high esteem this people who bears such a close resemblance to Jesus. The sight of the Jews as an oppressed and afflicted people crossing the face of the earth, despised and rejected, should make us think of those words of Jesus about the destitute and needy: 'Truly, I say to you, as you did it to one of the least of these my brethren, you did it to me' (Matthew 25:40). Who matches so accurately our Lord's description 'the least of these my brethren' as His people Israel? Who has suffered so much contempt from all nations down through the ages? Who has been so rejected? From whom did people turn away their faces? Who has been persecuted and tormented with such burning hatred? Who has been wounded and tortured to death so often as this, His people? Here, indeed, are the brethren of our Lord Jesus.

It may well be that He often feels closer to His people Israel than to those proud Christians who believe in Him and yet refuse to acknowledge their guilt towards the Jews, their heartlessness in passing by their brother in his desperate need. How far away they are from the Gospel, which can be summed up as: breaking down before God like the penitent tax-collector and confessing one's guilt in contrition, so receiving the grace of forgiveness.

One day Jesus will pronounce against such believers those fearful words: 'Depart from me, you cursed, into the eternal fire prepared for the devil and his angels' (Matthew 25:41). For it was the least of His brethren who were allowed to starve to death, who were refused shelter in their desperate fear when they were about to be sent to their death, who were not clothed in their abject poverty, who when sick and in prison were not visited while this was still possible.

How few Christians maintained a cordial, brotherly relationship with their Jewish fellow-citizens out of love for Jesus! How seldom did they stand protectively in front of their elder brother when he was humiliated and slandered! Yet there is only one standard that is valid before God: 'If you know these things, blessed are you if you do them' (John 13:17); 'A doer that acts, he shall be blessed in his doing' (James 1:25).

The Lord Jesus is interested in our doing, and one day He will declare to all those who said, 'Lord, Lord', but failed to do the will of the Father in heaven, however much they 'believed' in Jesus, 'I never knew you' (Matthew 7:21ff.). It could be that He will not be able to show us mercy because we have passed His people by, although we call

Him the source of our forgiveness and justification. And it could be that He will pronounce His woes on us instead: 'You say, I am rich, I have prospered, and I need nothing; not knowing that you are wretched, pitiable, poor, blind, and naked' (Revelation 3:17).

Perhaps this woe has long since been pronounced on us. Such a woe pronounced by Jesus is a dreadful verdict. The poor and those who weep here are called blessed by Jesus. If poor Lazarus was carried to Abraham's bosom (Luke 16:22), should not these millions of Jews who breathed their last amid circumstances of untold cruelty also be comforted in Abraham's bosom? Are they not Lazarus? And we are the rich ones before whose gate he lay — we who had everything, we who were not outcasts. He desired to live from our crumbs; yet he was not allowed to live, because he had not found in us one thing: mercy. There was no mercy, because we, though calling ourselves after the Lord of mercy, knew nothing of merciful love.

Where was the good Samaritan when the Jews fell among the robbers? Where was the Christian Church, which is supposed to follow his example? Apart from the odd Christian here and there who secretly sheltered Jews in his home or helped them in other ways, the Christians in general failed in the hour of Israel's greatest need. It became evident that the Christian Church was not like Jesus nor a true disciple of His. Instead of acting like the good Samaritan, it passed by on the other side like the priest and the Levite (Luke 10). We know that Jesus pronounced His woe upon the scribes and Pharisees. That woe is also upon us.

There is only one thing we can do now: cast ourselves down at the Father's feet like the prodigal son and confess, 'I am no longer worthy to be called your son' (Luke 15:21). We have not even dimly reflected the nature of God our Father, the essence of which is merciful love. This attribute His people has not found in us.

How are the Jews to believe in Jesus? Have not we ourselves blindfolded them? They cannot see Jesus because of our conduct. They cannot believe in Him, because in our lives we have not presented to them the image of Jesus; rather we have shown them the image of mercilessness. 'Your deeds in Germany talk so loud that I cannot hear your words,' a Jew of our times commented. Our words about Jesus must cut the Jews to the heart, considering the cruelties we have perpetrated against them in the name of this Jesus from the time of the Crusades up to the present day. And not only that. How many acts of love have we neglected to do? Thus we share in the horrible guilt of our people in murdering six million Jews. This guilt still hovers over us all like a dark cloud.

Chapter 5

The Extent of German Guilt

C AN WE GERMANS really continue to walk under the open sky of our fatherland, in daytime in the sunshine and at night beneath the stars, enjoying it all without feelings of shame? Must we not always remember that not long ago, under that same sky, in the midst of our people, gigantic flames ascended from the burning bodies of millions of people day and night? Were not these flames like a cry of desperation and a raised finger of accusation? Indeed, having witnessed these crimes, the sun ought to veil its face, and the stars refuse to shine. But it was not only the sun, the stars and the heavens; the heart of God the Father had to witness it all. What unimaginable pain it must have caused Him when He looked down and saw the horrors of the concentration camps, all those desperate people, who were His creatures, children of His and members of His beloved chosen people!

Here demonized men, obsessed with hatred for God, created a hell for their fellow-men. Now we know what it must be like in hell, the domain of Satan. Holy Scripture depicts it as a place where there is wailing and gnashing of teeth. Reading factual reports of the extermination camps, we can have some conception of hell. Do we believe now that hell actually exists? If we reckon with reward we shall.

If Satan's henchmen here on earth, who designed these camps and ran them, could devise and construct such an inferno, what must hell itself be like under its prince and ruler? Those who served him here will have to serve him there. There they will reap what they have sown here. For them it will be a hundredfold or millionfold Auschwitz for all eternity.

If our Lord Jesus rewards a hundredfold those who, for His sake, have left all and have suffered for Him, Satan also will reward his servants. But we know what his rewards are like. The reward for those who serve him here is that he appears as their accuser and takes them with him into his fearful domain to torment them from eternity to eternity. Considering the burning ovens of the death camps, those hellish fires inspired by Satan in our times, does it still surprise us that medieval man depicted hell as a place of constant burning and of ascending smoke?

'All transient things are merely symbolic,' Goethe once said. All that is done and created in the name of God is symbolic of what God the Father does. It is symbolic of His love, His kindnesses, the joys He has prepared. It is symbolic of the heavenly world and the Father's house. But what is done in Satan's name by people who are hostile towards God is symbolic of what it is like in the realm of hell.

We Germans were Satan's henchmen. In the midst of our people this hell was created. After reading the reports of those who survived it, we can only confess that never before in the whole span of history has a civilized nation been guilty of a crime such as has been committed here in Germany, a Christian country, a land of culture. Here Satan was able to set up his rule and construct hellish places, such as never before had existed. Within a few years, millions of people were murdered, gassed, burnt alive or tortured to death in every conceivable way. Who can still eat his fill at a nicely laid table without visualizing the emaciated forms of the thousands of victims in the extermination camps?

A. Hochhäuser reports on these horrors in *Unter dem gelben Stern*:

> The train that was to take us to Buchenwald was shunted on to a side track, and soon the pitiful transport of half-starved people was on its way. Our spirits were very low. After a two-hour journey we arrived at our destination; that is, for the last part of the way we had to walk. When we reached the camp we were completely exhausted and worn out. The pangs of hunger were by now almost unbearable, and the bitter cold filled our cup of misery to overflowing. We hoped we were now at last to find a bed for our weary bodies.

> In our ten thousands we stood on the vast parade ground, a whole city of misery. Buchenwald at that time lodged about sixty thousand persons, and it was inconceivable that this number could be doubled there and then. We had

to wait and wait without anything being done for our relief. It was three whole days before we were admitted to be deloused. We received neither food nor water, and daily thousands perished.

The medical orderlies worked non-stop. The crematorium also worked without pause. Soon corpses were piled up like mountains. Several were there who had paid with their lives for struggling to be deloused more quickly. We were stuffed into large bath-tubs filled with disinfectant. Many died in these baths. The countless sores burned like fire as soon as they came into contact with the hot disinfectant, and the pain was frightful. After being deloused, we were then clothed. We were given wooden clogs with rags for the feet, a shirt, a pair of linen trousers and a linen jacket. Since it was February and still cold, this kind of clothing offered scarcely any protection against the weather. At last we received the long-awaited first ration of food in the Buchenwald concentration camp. To those of us who were still strong enough to receive the food it gave new strength. But others were too weak even for this and they died before their turn came. In the morning the bodies of those who had died of starvation were lying in front of every hut, ready to be taken to the crematorium by the 'heaven transporters'.

In our rooms the beds were not even planks but more like shelves in tiers, reminding us of those in warehouses. Blankets or anything of the kind were completely unknown. But to secure even so primitive a resting-place as that was not too easy. If anyone was not in the block on time after roll call, he was forced to lie down all night on the bare floor or lean against the wall.

Apart from the prisoners' barracks there was in Buchenwald a large S.S. school and a dog-training centre in which dogs were trained to tear human beings to pieces...

Buchenwald was hell on earth...When the Allies marched in, they found hundreds of corpses and the dying reduced to skeletons. For example, of six hundred Norwegian Jews who were in Buchenwald since 1942, only one survived to be liberated.

And this is what we have done, we Germans! None can exonerate himself from blame. Collective guilt is a reality. Daniel, in his prayer of repentance, asks God to forgive him his sin and the sin of his people (Daniel 9:16ff.), although he had been one of those who were loyal to God and kept His commandments. But as a member of his people, Daniel had to accept their guilt as his own. Similarly, we cannot dissociate ourselves from our family when one member commits a crime. Instead we can only express grief and dismay that such a thing could happen in our family. We feel ashamed and because we, too, feel responsible we try to make good, if possible, the damage caused by that member's wrongdoing. How much more should this apply to our relationship with our nation? Certainly, no one can relieve us of this shame, as the President of the West German

Federal Republic, Theodor Heuss, stated on the occasion of the unveiling of the memorial in Bergen-Belsen concentration camp.

Yet it is not enough to acknowledge our collective guilt because of our people's deeds, which have brought us shame and dishonour before all other nations and before every morally sensitive and civilized person. We are personally to blame. We all have to admit that if we, the entire Christian community, had stood up as one man and if, after the burning of the synagogues, we had gone out on the streets and voiced our disapproval, rung the church bells, and somehow boycotted the actions of the S.S., the devil's vassals would probably not have been at such liberty to pursue their evil schemes. But we lacked the ardour of love — love that is never passive, love that cannot bear it when its fellow-men are in misery, particularly when they are subjected to such appalling treatment and tortured to death. Indeed, if we had loved God, we would not have endured seeing those houses of God set ablaze; rather, our souls would have been filled with holy, divine wrath. We were lukewarm, and to the lukewarm the Lord says, 'I will spew you out of my mouth' (Revelation 3:16). By their apathy the lukewarm can make themselves more blameworthy in the sight of God than those who are actively engaged in wrongdoing. The latter, in their evil doings, can perhaps be more easily convicted of their sins than the lukewarm.

Oh, that we as Germans and as Christians would stand aghast and cry out ever anew, 'What have we done!' At every further evidence of our guilt may we repeat the cry. Not only men and women belonging to God's people but children, countless numbers of innocent, little children, were slaughtered in the most fiendish manner. Let us listen again to Lucie Adelsberger:

According to S.S. regulations, every Jewish child automatically brought death to its mother. The concentration camp did not accept Jewish children. Apart from the few who escaped detection, they were thrown, living or gassed, into the fire upon arrival. Not only the children but the mothers too. Every woman who had a child with her, even if it was not her own but another's whom she happened to be looking after, was doomed to death. The older and more experienced prisoners often tried at the ramp to push the children away from the mothers to the grandmothers, who anyway were doomed to be gassed because of their age. It was heart-rending to see mothers who did not want to be separated from their children snatch them back, not knowing — though many did know — that it would mean that they would die together, and to hear the men in the first days after their arrival inquire anxiously after their wives and children.

Pregnant women often arrived in the camp. Some of them were forced to have an abortion, even in the fourth or fifth month, with no regard for the hazards entailed in terminating a pregnancy at that stage ... Pregnant Jewish women who on arrival had escaped the gas chamber, and who did not have an abortion, were delivered of their children. They were, as far as this was possible in the concentration camp, under medical supervision and received nursing care, and the delivery took place in the normal way. As soon as the little infant, however, had opened its eyes to the light of this world, the unbelievable occurred. The Jewish child was doomed to death and the mother with it. Within one week both went to the gas chamber.

Oh, who can now look upon German children playing happily and not think of the many, many thousands of children who screamed in anguish and terror when they were burnt alive or when, either with or without their parents, they choked to death in the gas chambers! May we not close our eyes but face up to what we have done, for these are the plain facts, and innocent blood cries for retribution: 'If any one slays with the sword, with the sword must he be slain' (Revelation 13:10). Thus says Holy Scripture.

Chapter 6

God's Answer and Our Reaction

D O WE REALIZE that in keeping with God's righteousness, we German people are all doomed to die because of what we have done — slaughtering millions of innocent people in the most brutal fashion? Do we realize that God's sword of judgment hangs over us and will fall upon us without fail if we do not repent and obtain forgiveness for our sins?

Divine retribution has already begun to catch up with us. In a small measure we have received our deserts. Did we not set the synagogues on fire, and afterwards churches almost all over the country went up in flames? We thrust the Jews from their homes, so that they had to flee under cruellest circumstances; later, long columns of German refugees trekked across the land. By forcing Jews to emigrate and by deporting them, we tore families mercilessly apart; and now the Iron Curtain separates our people, tearing families apart. We buried Jews alive and, under crumbling houses, Germans were buried alive. Yes, the judgment that has come upon us in the form of massive bombings and the invasion of our country, is God's answer to the atrocities we have committed against His chosen people. Yet it is an answer nowhere near the punishment we deserve because of our crimes. God is still giving us time to repent.

What further judgments, then, await us? God is holy and His law is irrevocable. It is a spiritual truth that man is punished by the very things by which he sins. We prepared a hell for millions of people who were fellow-citizens of ours, who served our people, even laying down their lives on the battlefield. Does not justice demand that we experience hell on earth ourselves? Yes, a dark night of destruction, calamity and death will overtake Germany as God's judgment — if we do not repent. Just as millions of Jews perished cruelly, so millions of Germans will perish cruelly when barbarous hordes march through our land, setting up concentration camps after the same pattern and subjecting vast numbers to a painful death. Has not the Lord said that He Himself would be the avenger of His people and crush the nations (Isaiah 63:4,6)? Moreover, He said to Israel,

> I will contend with those who contend with you, and your children I will save. I will make your oppressors eat their own flesh ... Then all mankind will know that I, the Lord, am your Saviour, your Redeemer, the Mighty One of Jacob.
>
> Isaiah 49:25f. NIV

Yes, the Scriptures state clearly that His people shall live, whereas the nations shall perish, and first to do so will be those nations which have afflicted Israel. He who touches the apple of His eye must die, because he has attacked God Himself. Again and again God stresses His union with

His people, calling them His wife, His elect, His beloved.

Because of our national crime against Israel and thus against God Himself, we are still under judgment. And whenever we see anything to do with the Jews, whenever we meet them, whenever we hear of them, whether here or in the state of Israel — each Jew is a finger pointing to our guilt, even in his silence, for he is marked with countless wounds that we have inflicted on him, wounds of body and soul.

Beside every German stands, invisibly, a Jewish brother, one who has already passed into the realm of the dead, or one of the survivors, but each marked with terror and death — and each of them accuses us. Who can acquit us of such guilt? Only Jesus, our Saviour, can acquit us — provided that we have broken down at the cross with tears of repentance. Jesus Christ acquits only the sinner with a broken and contrite heart. The curse of judgment is cancelled only if there is repentance.

What are we to do in view of all this? Repent. The first step is to acknowledge our guilt. Then we need to show by our actions that we are filled with contrition for what happened, making amends precisely where we have failed. This is exemplified by John the Baptist's instructions to those who had taken advantage of others. As a mark of genuine repentance, they were to be all the more generous in giving away their possessions: 'He who has two coats, let him share with him who has none' (Luke 3:11).

In the Old Testament we read about the provision of the guilt offering. For instance, whoever had transgressed by defrauding another was required to return the defrauded goods along with the fifth part of their value (Leviticus 6:2ff.).

Considering how grievously we have failed to show love, do not we, the people of the New Testament, feel constrained by the love of Christ to show a hundredfold love and kindness to our Jewish brothers and fellow-citizens?

To be sure, we cannot really make up for what we have done. The individual survivors, many now living in Israel and trying to build up an existence for themselves, are for ever wounded and scarred in the depths of their hearts, because their relatives, parents, wives, children, brothers and sisters — often ten to twenty of them — have been cruelly murdered. We cannot restore them alive, even if we were to offer our own lives in exchange. Nor can we ever heal the wounds or undo the bestiality these people have suffered. We cannot remove the pain from their hearts. We cannot do more than pour oil on their wounds. But this we can do. Failure to do so shows that we have not yet allowed God to convict us of our guilt and are still not living in a state of repentance. If we do not feel drawn now towards our fellow Jewish citizens, or towards the Jews living in Israel, to show them all the kindness we can, then God's judgment continues to rest upon us and we provoke Him to deal out the heaviest blow yet upon our people.

We all live in dread of a nuclear war and the untold devastation in which it will result. Which country will suffer the most? The future lies in the hands of the holy God and Judge, and He judges justly. Woe betide us in Germany if there is not widespread repentance, especially among the Christians, because of the atrocities we have committed and the extent of our guilt! In the coming divine judgment we shall then be the ones to suffer.

It is a fact that those countries that offered refuge to the Jews and cared for them were spared the worst ravages of World War II. Does this not give us food for thought? Take Denmark, for instance. Together with their king, they rose as one man and bravely resisted the anti-Semitic measures ordered by Hitler, identifying themselves with the Jewish cause and conveying the Jews to safety in Sweden. For us who have sinned grievously against Israel, there is only one course of action left. If we do not want to reap what we have sown, we need to repent today so that our guilt can be atoned for.

What is meant by 'atoned for'? In Isaiah 27:9 we read, 'By this, then, will Jacob's [Israel's] guilt be atoned for' (NIV). In what way? By Israel going into exile and captivity. Israel has to atone for her guilt in that she suffers the consequences of her sinning, enduring the punishment.

Here God speaks of an atonement made by man, although Israel knew that her guilt could be removed only by the expiatory sacrifice where blood flowed. The fact that our guilt has been atoned for by Jesus does not exempt us Christians either from suffering the consequences of our sinning. We should be willing to bear punishment for our personal guilt as well as, in greater measure, for the sins of our people. God is looking for those who will 'stand in the breach'. He waits for such souls (Ezekiel 22:30). For their sake He can spare our people and prevent us from being delivered to judgment, just as He would have spared Sodom and Gomorrah for the sake of a righteous few. Yet whoever still has blood on his hands, unwept for, whoever refuses to be convicted of our crime against the Jews, lacks authority to pray that God will protect our people from further afflictions. As it is written:

> When you spread forth your hands [in prayer], I will hide my eyes from you; even though you make many prayers, I will not listen; your hands are full of blood. Wash yourselves; make yourselves clean; remove the evil of your doings from before my eyes; cease to do evil, learn to do good.
> Isaiah 1:15ff.

But if, following the prompting of the Holy Spirit, we accept divine judgment and endure it; if for the sake of our personal and national guilt towards Israel we humble ourselves beneath the mighty hand of God, which is stretched out in judgment against us as a nation; and if, thinking of Israel, we readily submit to His chastenings and judgments in our personal lives: we may have the assurance that this will be acceptable to God. It will follow naturally that where we have done evil we shall now feel constrained to do good.

Chapter 7

*God Waits in Vain
for Repentance*

STILL GOD WAITS, mostly in vain, for repentance among our people. Accordingly, His hand is still stretched out over us in wrath and judgment and not in blessing. The river of our tears of repentance should first flow over the mass graves of the Jews; then God could forgive us our sins; then our guilt would be atoned for, covered by the grace of God. For where sin increases, grace abounds all the more. Grace is bestowed where sinners shed tears of repentance and, driven by contrition, mend their ways and do good.

But how can we flee His wrath and where can we hide from the wrath of the living God so long as this condition is not fulfilled? Even if we were to go to 'the uttermost parts of the sea', there too His hand would lay hold of us, and at every turn His call would reach us: 'Where is your brother Abel? — Where is your brother Israel? — Where is he?' Then God would point to Auschwitz, Treblinka, Maidanek, Belzec, Gross-Rosen, Sobibor, where the smoking chimneys stood. To this day the camps can be seen where these our brothers have endured the horrors of hell. And God would say, 'Here is your brother Abel. I require his blood from your hand, you German people!' If Cain did not find any rest day or night because he murdered his brother, how can we Germans expect to find rest?

From Cain's words, 'My punishment is greater than I can bear' (Genesis 4:13), it is evident that he did not attain to repentance. If only we Germans would at least admit that our sin is great! But most of us do not even see or recognize the extent of our guilt. How, otherwise, could it be possible that the Christian Church, after all these atrocities, still remains so indifferent towards Israel? Should we not all hang our heads in shame? How can we still look a Jewish brother in the eye after all we have done to his people? But, strange to say, in this crucial matter we have lost all sense of honour and shame. We have no real awareness of this appalling sin, although we Protestants talk so much of sin and justification and of pardoned sinners. For all our knowledge we do not really know the meaning of sin, forgiveness and justification. We do not know that it is we who are sinners and in need of repentance, that it is we who are dependent on the grace of God and His forgiveness.

Because we are unaware of our sin, we do not seek forgiveness. Therefore, our guilt still rests upon us as a crushing weight. And because we are not willing to submit to God's verdict on our guilty nation, we are not ready to accept punishment and chastening and to humble ourselves beneath the mighty hand of God when He deals a blow to us and our people.

In the coming world war let us bear in mind that we are only receiving our just reward when calamity overtakes us. If we had but the faintest notion of our guilt as individuals and as a nation, we would repent. If we had but a glimmering of the truth, we could not meet our Jewish brothers without wanting to fall down before them in spirit and beg forgiveness. We would be deeply ashamed to think that we Germans have committed this heinous crime against them. In Germany have we not prided ourselves on being a people that stands for law and justice? Yet we are the ones who remained silent in the face of such injustice, whereas the Danish people took action and protected the Jews.

And even supposing that we remained silent because we dreaded that we should be thrown into concentration camp and there meet with a horrible death, should we not be ashamed of our cowardice now? Do not our consciences smite us after we have learnt of the Jews' suffering, brought on by our silence, of the extent of their persecution, of the diabolical passions let loose against them and of the barbarity to which they were subjected? Are we not shaken to the depths of our souls? Should we not break down under the immeasurable guilt we Germans have heaped upon ourselves?

Yet at Christian conferences and elsewhere how seldom grief is voiced, and our national crime deplored! Where are the troubled consciences? Where are the large repentance gatherings? Where is the church that regularly holds prayers of repentance for our crime against Israel? We pray for revivals, but they fail to come. A curse lies upon the Christian community, the curse of unrepented guilt towards Israel.

What has been done to atone for our guilt? Where are those who submit to God's verdict, not because they are forced to but of their own free will, and who on account of this guilt have served His people gladly and with sacrificial love? Where are those who humble themselves so deeply under their guilt like the great sinner (Luke 7) that, overwhelmed by the gift of forgiveness, they are filled with an overflowing love for God and their fellowmen, and particularly for those against whom they have sinned? A sign of the true life born of forgiveness is the outpouring of a great love. Who is there among our people who has already received this forgiveness in answer to genuine repentance for our great guilt towards Israel?

There cannot be many, for rarely does one hear that the Jews have become especially beloved; that they have been showered with kindnesses; that time, money, and all that one values and holds dear are sacrificed for them. Rather, we tend to show embarrassment and lovelessness towards our Jewish brethren now living among us again. We pay no attention to them. We do not help them. We allow them to be slighted, saying nothing when they once again become the object of scorn. It is also a fact that in various places Jewish cemeteries are still as uncared for now as in the days of Hitler because the Jewish communities have almost completely disappeared and there are very few among our guilt-laden people who are prepared to be responsible for their upkeep.

Rather, time and again sacrilegious hands have caused damage.

That this attitude prevails is borne out by another fact. There are still many Jews waiting for restitution payments and who for this reason have to live in the most unfavourable conditions, especially in Paris, with no one to care for them. Should not people in Germany seize with both hands this opportunity of proffering money and gifts to improve the lot, however slightly, of our Jewish brethren? But how many of those who as a result of maltreatment are maimed for life or suffering from incurable complaints wait in vain for a helping hand? In view of all this there is no excuse for lack of personal involvement. We are not justified in leaning comfortably upon the official state reparations, for this is no more than a normal debt of honour of any constitutional state and does not absolve us from the personal, inner responsibility before God for our treatment of our Jewish brethren.

How much has been sacrificed among Christians for Israel's new homeland, which is now being developed with such painstaking effort? If genuine repentance and the desire for making amends had been aroused among the Christian churches, should not every Christian have been inspired to donate at least one olive tree, the vital 'constructional unit' of Israel's afforestation? We could also find other ways of aiding the development of Israel seeing that there are numerous institutions that can be supported by voluntary contributions.

Chapter 8

Judgment Is Impending

I F NOW, after the extent of our national crime has come to light, we remain blind, unrepentant and indifferent towards those we have afflicted, we continue to heap guilt upon ourselves against the day of our judgment. At this point one can only cry out, 'Awake, awake, O German people!' The fearful judgment of God is impending. But just as Israel in the Old Testament again and again disregarded the warnings of divine judgment, so we too do not want to believe that judgment will descend. Yet we have Israel as a proof, a visible sign, that every word of God comes true. With our own eyes we can see how, according to the promise, the Jews are returning from the dispersion into the land of their fathers. Previously, we also saw how the threatened judgment of dispersion was fulfilled as a result of their disobedience. With equal precision the promises and curses that God has pronounced on those who deal with Israel are being fulfilled: blessing on those who bless Israel and show goodness to her; and judgment on those who cause her any hurt or destruction. The Word of God cannot fail. What He says is Yea and Amen and will come to pass at the appointed time.

When will the sword of divine judgment descend? We may assume that this day is not far off. Do we not wish to do all we can to avert a war between the two Germanys, a war which looms like a spectre before our eyes? The hand of the Lord can be stayed if He finds people who submit to His verdict beforehand, repent and atone for their sins. How many such people would it take for God to refrain from destroying Germany? That we do not know. But one thing we do know is that the number of those who are currently living in such a state of repentance, atoning for their sin, and showing love to Israel wherever they can is infinitesimal and scarcely deserves mention. Yet the Lord is waiting for the completion of a certain number who are willing to be convicted and to atone for the sin-stained past.

Yes, God is waiting. He is waiting with infinite patience. For so many years now He has waited for our repentance. Should we not do all we can now to rejoice the Father's heart with our repentance? If there is joy in heaven with Him who is heaven's Lord and with His angels when a soul repents, how much more so when we Christians at last come to repentance for what we have done to His people!

How long will God continue to wait? There is a limit to His patience and then comes judgment. Who can count the brief years, who can count the months, the days, that are still given to us for repentance? So long as the time of grace lasts we still have the opportunity to repent and atone for our sins. Destruction will come suddenly

(1 Thessalonians 5:3), and then it will be too late to repent.

This is a critical issue, involving every one of us personally, for at our death we shall stand before the judgment seat of God and the question about His chosen people will be put to us. Then we shall be, inescapably, delivered up to Him and His verdict. Every one of us will have to face the question about our treatment of the Jews, about what we have done or not done to these our brothers.

So long as we are on earth, judgment can be turned into grace if we repent — but not after we have died. Then judgment will bring us con-demnation from which there is no escaping and from which no excuse can save us. Whoever, therefore, wishes to find grace before the Lord, whoever loves Germany and wishes to help save her from destruction — let him join the ranks of those who are willing to be convicted of their sins here and now and to make amends. But, above all, whoever loves God and does not wish to provoke or grieve Him any longer, let him repent today and confess his guilt, so that the grace of forgiveness may be poured out upon him. Let him show love and kindness to our Jewish brethren while there is still time.

PART TWO

*The Turning-Point in God's
Plan for Israel:
God's Challenge to the
Nations*

Chapter 9

The First Phase in
the New Era

A TURNING-POINT in redemptive history has arrived. Could it be that Israel's eyes are quicker to see this than the eyes of Christians? At a gathering of four hundred Zionists in July 1957, Israel's Prime Minister, David Ben-Gurion, declared, 'Two thousand years have we waited for this moment and now it is here. When the fullness of time has come, no one can withstand God.' With Israel's return, one of the greatest miracles of world history has occurred: a people without land, kings, princes or temple for almost two thousand years, dispersed among all nations, a people mercilessly persecuted down through the ages and repeatedly threatened with extermination-policies, culminating in the 'final solution' of the most recent past — this people, scattered like 'dry bones' throughout the world, has overnight been reassembled as a nation and has become visible as a state.

Had not Israel a short while ago received her death-blow in Germany? Yet this Israel lives; she has emerged as a people and established a state. Before our very eyes a truly great miracle of God is taking place in divine history, all in fulfilment of what the Lord has said:

> Who has heard such a thing? Who has seen such
> things? Shall a land be born in one day? Shall a
> nation be brought forth in one moment? For as
> soon as Zion was in labour she brought forth her
> sons.   Isaiah 66:8

The people of Israel recognize this miracle and praise God for it.

When on February 17, 1949, Chaim Weizmann was solemnly inducted into the office of President of the State of Israel, he exclaimed with tears, 'Let us praise and thank the God of Israel, who has graciously delivered us out of centuries of affliction and suffering! The world stops to listen whether a new message will go forth from Zion.' In an address given at the Zionist Congress, in 1956, David Ben-Gurion said, after stressing that 'the state of Israel is instrumental to the realization of the Messianic vision', and that 'the state needs to advocate the concept of redemption': 'We live in the Messianic age. The return of the Jews to their land is the beginning of the realization of the Messianic vision.'

Yes, Israel is aware that a major turning-point in redemptive history has arrived. She experiences and sees that the time of dispersion, and with it her time of greatest judgment, is coming to an end and that the scripture is being fulfilled:

> Though I removed them far off among the nations,
> and though I scattered them among the coun-
> tries ... I will gather you from the peoples, and
> assemble you out of the countries where you have
> been scattered, and I will give you the land of
> Israel.   Ezekiel 11:16f.

The hour has come when God, having previously hidden His face, now turns towards Israel again. The hour of grace is dawning for His people. Of course, this is only the beginning; many of His promises have yet to be fulfilled. What is now happening is only the first part of what the prophets have foretold about the return of the people of Israel.

According to Holy Scripture, this return consists of two phases. We know that Ezekiel first speaks of the coming together of the 'dry bones' (Ezekiel 37), in other words, of a physical return to the land of Israel. Then comes the second phase, in which the Spirit of God must enter the dry bones. The physical return will culminate in the spiritual return of the people to their God. This will be the hour when they are accepted. We read in Romans 11:15,

> If their rejection means the reconciliation of the world, what will their acceptance mean but life from the dead?

Their acceptance will be so great a blessing to all nations and to the Christian Church that it is described as 'life from the dead'. As already said, the rebirth of the state of Israel, the physical return of the Jews, only recently the victims of a policy of extermination, is the first great miracle, paving the way for this 'life from the dead'.

How much more wonderful it will be when the second miracle comes to pass and they are awakened spiritually! Then they will draw the nations after them; then will dawn the day of redemption for all the nations of the world:

> It shall come to pass in the latter days that the
> mountain of the house of the Lord shall be estab-
> lished as the highest of the mountains, and shall
> be raised up above the hills; and peoples shall flow
> to it.
>
> Micah 4:1

However fervent our longing for this second
phase, we must not overlook the significance of
the first phase, Israel's physical return. When
God pronounced upon Israel the covenant blessings and curses (Zechariah 8:13), He was address-
ing her as an earthly people, guaranteeing her a
heritage on earth. This means that the first phase
of the major turning-point in God's plan for Israel
is connected with her land. The promises given
through the prophets make it very clear that the
regathering and redemption of the Jewish people
will take place in Erez Israel and only there. As
part of His covenant with Abraham, God gave
him the Promised Land as a possession for his
descendants:

> He is mindful of his covenant for ever, of the word
> that he commanded, for a thousand generations,
> the covenant which he made with Abraham, his
> sworn promise to Isaac, which he confirmed to
> Jacob as a statute, to Israel as an everlasting
> covenant, saying, 'To you I will give the land of
> Canaan as your portion for an inheritance.'
>
> Psalm 105:8ff.

The covenant of God with Abraham and His
people does not speak of a possession and inheritance in heaven; rather, it refers to the land of
Canaan, which God Himself has granted Israel in
the covenant He made with her as a people living
on earth. All the biblical prophecies about the

regathering of dispersed Israel declare that she shall be brought back to her own country, the land of her fathers, the land of Canaan, which was promised to Abraham. There 'the Lord will inherit Judah as his portion in the holy land, and will again choose Jerusalem' (Zechariah 2:12).

Accordingly, the state of Israel in the land of Canaan has a very special calling, a unique and eternally significant one, for at the heart of this calling is an everlasting covenant. To be sure, the state of Israel does not yet manifest the Kingdom of God on earth, which is the ultimate fulfilment of this calling. Only when Israel recognizes her Messiah when He reveals Himself to her and only when He establishes His royal rule, will something of the Kingdom of God on earth become visible there. Jerusalem, 'the beloved city' and 'the camp of the saints' (Revelation 20:9), will then be the centre of this Kingdom of God on earth, which will precede the coming of the new world. Seeing this, all the other nations will then submit to the rule of God and worship Him.

Thus Israel is the people of God's choice, and she will always be His choice and the object of His love. To the chosen people is allocated the Promised Land, where the Kingdom of God is to be established. No matter what struggles and afflictions may come, it will remain Israel's possession, for 'the gifts and the call of God are irrevocable'. Indeed, God affirms the promise to His people that upon their return they will possess the land for ever: 'I will plant them upon their land, and they shall never again be plucked

up out of the land which I have given them'
(Amos 9:15).

A state of Israel is inseparably bound up with the
land of the fathers, Canaan. It can never be at any
other place. This was demonstrated at the Sixth
Zionist Congress, in 1903, when Theodor Herzl
conveyed to the Jews the offer to establish the Jewish state in Uganda, East Africa. All pious Jews,
particularly those from Russia, began to weep and
lament in deep distress and refused to go there.
Jerusalem alone was in their hearts. The Holy Land,
the Promised Land that God had promised them,
was the object of their longing — only there could
they 'return home'. For almost two thousand years
they had been offering their daily prayers to God
with yearning and tears that He would lead them
back home to Zion. Only there could they, as Jews,
live and die in 'their' land. And now that their
homecoming has become a reality, settlements in
Israel often bear the name of Zion: 'Shavei Zion',
'Rishon le-Zion', 'Nes Ziyyonah'.

In Israel today there is a renewed awareness
that this land is a gift of God and is closely
connected with His divine purposes. So literally
does David Ben-Gurion take the allotment and
boundaries of the land laid down by God in
the Holy Scriptures that he would not dare to
encroach upon a neighbouring country like Egypt,
simply because God has commanded His people
not to return to Egypt. 'This commandment not to
return to Egypt was given to us when we left that
country 3,300 years ago. Therefore, our military
operations [autumn 1956] were entirely limited

to the territory of the Sinai Peninsula' (address before the Knesset, the parliament of Israel, November 8, 1956).

What other nation can say, in the context of wars and political affairs, 'We have been told, not by man, but by God, the living God!'

> He declares his word to Jacob, his statutes and ordinances to Israel. He has not dealt thus with any other nation.   Psalm 147:19f.

This has become visible again. Today there actually exists a people who include the name of God in their governmental affairs to such an extent that one feels, 'This is the people of God!' A state has come into existence, unique in its kind, because it is based on the Holy Scriptures of the Old Testament. For its emblem it has the menorah, the seven-branched candelabra, flanked by two olive branches, a symbol taken from the Holy Scriptures (Zechariah 4:2f.). David Ben-Gurion, Prime Minister of Israel, speaks publicly of the miracles of God taking place today in Israel and of the beginning of the realization of the Messianic vision.

Apart from Israel, there has never been on this earth a nation who as a whole has lived and lives under the rule of God and who takes the laws and commandments of God as binding for its state. What distinguishes the people of Israel is that their legislation for family, culture and state is not of human origin but of direct divine origin. As it is written in Deuteronomy 4:8, 'What great nation is there, that has statutes and ordinances so righteous as all this law which I set before you this day?' (cf. 2 Samuel 7:23; 1 Chronicles 17:21f.).

It is of the greatest significance that God has promised His people their land as an everlasting possession. Only if His people dwell together again in their own land can a state exist, whose government can rule according to the ordinances of Holy Scripture. Yes, here is a nation that openly takes its stand on the Word of God. Today the Bible is the book of the Israelis, and for many it is more contemporary and valid than the Talmud. In radio broadcasts, at youth gatherings, in the home and on the street, scriptural texts are frequently quoted. By taking the Word of God seriously, His people have begun to demonstrate their special relationship to God, who in turn reveals again His special relationship to them as 'a father to Israel' (Jeremiah 31:9). He endorses the election of Israel in Abraham, which includes the promise of the land and of earthly gifts.

Israel's election is not temporal but for ever. It is as certain as His promise that day and night will not cease. It is as unchangeable as the firmly established ordinances regulating the phases of the moon and the orbits of the stars. God has solemnly sworn this to His people (Jeremiah 31:35f.; 33:25f.). And this election has endured for the past two thousand years in spite of the fall of the ancient Jewish state (AD 70), and despite the fact that Israel during these two millennia was a people without her own land, government or temple.

That this election continues to be valid is furthermore attested by the fact that the Jews have retained the individuality of their language and religion to this day. At the World Congress of Jewish Studies, in September 1957, Jewish and non-Jewish scholars were assigned the task of explaining why the cultures of ancient civilizations of the Near East, such as Egypt and Babylon, disappeared, whereas the language and literature of the Jews were preserved throughout four thousand years of uninterrupted tradition and are even now undergoing a revival. This could happen only because Holy Scripture, and thus God Himself, is their unshakeable foundation. Only because God Himself stands behind the rebirth of the state of Israel at this turning-point in divine history could it come into existence in the land of Canaan.

Chapter 10

A Danger
Again Threatening the
Christian World

THE CONFLICT connected with the land of Canaan is of the greatest significance, not only for Israel but also for the Christian world. Will the latter see the purposes of God behind current events? Once again Christendom is in danger of blindly opposing the Word of God and His promises to Israel, and ultimately His covenant and plan of salvation. This would amount to perpetuating the guilt of past centuries against Israel, and thereby against God Himself, and bringing it to a further climax. If God Himself has made a covenant with His people to give them this land as an inheritance for ever, how then can the question be raised among Christians as to whether another people should possess this land today? The Lord says:

> I will bring them again each to his heritage and
> each to his land.   Jeremiah 12:15

> In your land you shall possess a double portion.
>   Isaiah 61:7

The land of Canaan has been given by God to His people as an everlasting inheritance. No other people has any right to this land but Israel alone, for God has said,

> I thought how I would set you among my sons, and give you a pleasant land, a heritage most beauteous of all nations.   Jeremiah 3:19

Anyone, therefore, who disputes Israel's right to the land of Canaan opposes God, His holy covenant with the patriarchs and His solemn utterances and promises.

We may recall the Balfour Declaration of 1917 in which was recognized, not by the Church but by statesmen, the historical right of the Jews to Palestine, a view reiterated in the 1922 Mandate, which stated: '... Recognition has ... been given to the historical connection of the Jewish people with Palestine and to the grounds for reconstituting their national home in that country.'

Even if we, in our blindness, do not recognize God's covenantal gift to Israel of the land of Canaan as an everlasting possession, ought not our Christian ethical sense promote in us the desire that Israel should be able to stay in her own land?

As in times past, Israel is among the nations today as the 'worm Jacob' (Isaiah 41:14), a small nation of two million, while her neighbours number forty million. Erez Israel is again the smallest country. Her territory is about the size of the German state of Hesse, whereas the nations surrounding her are in possession of vast tracts of land.

Today as thousands of years ago Israel is a small nation dwarfed by bigger nations and under constant threat of raids and wars. Since days of old

God has lovingly and compassionately regarded the hard lot of His people, and He has comforted them, saying, 'I will help you' (Isaiah 41:14). Yet we Christians, on the whole, have very little sympathy for this people in their dire distress. Many Christians have sympathy only for the surrounding nations that threaten tiny Israel, outnumber her and are superior to her in military strength and in the support they receive from other powers. This can only be because we no longer seriously accept the law of the Scriptures that God takes under His care the afflicted, poor and needy, coming to their aid. He draws near to him whom He sees lying there in his blood (Ezekiel 16:6). He has mercy on him who is without help.

We, as disciples of Jesus, should do likewise, for this is what the parable of the good Samaritan is all about. Yet we do not. We may have all kinds of reasons for our attitude, arguing, for instance, that other people too are in need. Certainly, hardships abound in other nations and we are lovingly to remember them in their afflictions because all are God's creatures. But if we sincerely want to follow God's commandment to love our neighbour as ourselves, our first obligation is to 'the man who fell among the robbers' (Luke 10:36) — the one who is in desperate need and in a state of utter helplessness. This is our neighbour, as Jesus points out very clearly. There can be no doubt who this is for us in Germany. It is Israel, the Jews, of whom some six million died at our hands. If we had but a dim perception of the extent of our guilt, we would be so conscience-stricken that we would now go out of our way to assist Israel and show her kindness, seeing that we have afflicted her so grievously.

But Israel receives next to no help from Christian churches and organizations — though her neighbours receive it. Dr. E. Rees, consultant on refugee affairs to the World Council of Churches, states that the Arab refugees are the only case to his knowledge where free-will gifts from organizations, particularly Christian ones, constitute more than one-third of the donations dispensed by the United Nations. In other words, donations from the Christian world amounting to millions have gone to the Arabs, though, to quote Dr. Rees, '. . . five years ago the General Assembly of the United Nations assigned the sum of 200 million dollars to build homes and create work for the Arab refugees. And though there are in the world at present 30 to 40 million refugees, only the 900 thousand Arabs are cared for and kept by international relief.' According to his statements, there would be sufficient room for the settlement of these refugees — plenty of land in Iraq and Syria, money (oil wells) and increasing employment opportunities.

In Israel's neighbouring states, which are hostile to her, there are men in influential positions who in former days were actively involved in the German National Socialist movement. They helped to exterminate the Jews among us, and now with undiminished hatred they seek to destroy the tiny nation building up its existence in Canaan. Do we not read and hear again the words Hitler used? — 'Israel must be annihilated.'

Yet with misguided compassion, we favour the enemies of the people of God, and our money flows to them. It is especially the Christian world and Christian magazines that repeatedly express sympathy for the misery of the Arab refugees, while no mention is made of the plight of our elder brother Israel. How is it that the greater distress of Israel leaves us unaffected? It is incomprehensible. Should not Israel be far closer to us, seeing that Jesus came from this people and that through the Jews we have received the law and the prophets? Yet the plight of this people who have suffered so terribly at our hands, against whom we have sinned so grievously, and who today have to struggle for survival and build up their country with enemies all around them, leaves us generally unmoved.

Now it is time to awake, for the last hour is near. If all the time we have been opposing God's people or else condoning the attacks made on them by powers hostile to God, woe betide us later when the whole world is caught up in a rebellion against God! Then, without even noticing it, we shall suddenly find ourselves on the side of the antichristian kingdom, whose prime target will be the Jews (Daniel 8).

The Jews are the hour hand on the clock of world history — so it has always been said. Moreover, our relationship with them is indicative of our true relationship to the Lord Jesus, showing whether it is a relationship of love. If we love Jesus, we shall love the people whom He loves and always will love and who will yet be the centre and blessing of all nations. The Word of God endures for ever. That which it declares will not fail to come to pass: 'Blessed be every one who blesses you, and cursed be every one who curses you' (Numbers 24:9), as we shall experience especially at the end of time. In the painful conflict concerning the Holy Land, may we be supportive towards the people of God. They are His elect and to them He has given the land of Canaan for an everlasting possession.

Chapter 11

Flimsy Excuses

WHO IN CHRISTENDOM will recognize the significant hour that has struck in divine history, and who will pass it by? It will soon be two thousand years since Christendom, as a whole, began passing by Israel, the people of God, in their dire need. In so doing, they have passed by Jesus Himself, whose image the Jews reflected. Are we going to do the same today? What hinders us from recognizing this vital point in history? It is the widespread erroneous view that Israel is cast off and that the Jews, therefore, can neither be restored to favour nor look forward to a day of salvation or resurrection. But God's Word says otherwise:

> Blindness in part is happened to Israel, until the fullness of the Gentiles be come in. And so all Israel shall be saved. Romans 11:25f. AV

Indeed, it cannot be otherwise, for with this people God has made an everlasting covenant. As long as the earth remains, it cannot be dissolved.

> My steadfast love shall not depart from you [Israel], and my covenant of peace shall not be removed, says the Lord, who has compassion on you.
> Isaiah 54:10

In this covenant the Lord has taken Israel as His wife and joined her to Himself, as He says:

Your Maker is your husband.

Isaiah 54:5; cf. Ezekiel 16:60

Though Israel has broken this marriage covenant again and again, God has never done so. Israel remains the beloved wife of God.

The Lord has called you like a wife forsaken and grieved in spirit, like a wife of youth when she is cast off, says your God.   Isaiah 54:6

All the expressions of divine love still hold good for Israel today. None of them are cancelled. Israel is and always will be the apple of God's eye (Zechariah 2:8). She remains God's joy and delight, His royal diadem (Isaiah 62:3), His firstborn, His chosen one, His beloved (Jeremiah 2:2; Hosea 11:1). Indeed, He says of His people, 'Like the jewels of a crown they shall shine on his land' (Zechariah 9:16).

Israel is and always will be the first-born son of God. Though the Jews have been two thousand years under God's chastening hand, they were no less precious to the Father during this time of judgment. And even if in the trials of the dispersion it appeared that the Jews were no longer beloved by God, in actual fact such times were a proof that they were dearly beloved as chosen ones of God. Only because God loved them did He chasten them.

A father is obliged to discipline his child, because all human beings are born in sin. A shadow then falls across the relationship between father and child. The father's heart is still full of love for his child, though his face becomes stern and he seems to be estranged from his child. All the time the father is just waiting for the moment when, having achieved his objective, he can once again show his love for his child and the shadow can be removed. Every child undergoing discipline is especially close to the heart of his father, who takes care that his child does not suffer further from another, unauthorized hand.

Similarly the Lord has watched carefully to see whether His afflicted people have been treated lovingly by us or not. We read in the Holy Scriptures:

> I was angry with my people, I profaned my heritage; I gave them into your hand, you showed them no mercy; on the aged you made your yoke exceedingly heavy.   Isaiah 47:6

Elsewhere He says:

> I am very angry with the nations that are at ease; for while I was angry but a little they furthered the disaster.   Zechariah 1:15

Even if heathen nations have dealt Israel too heavy a blow, how can we account for such treatment from Christian nations? The answer is that many Christians fail to recognize God's eternal purposes concerning Israel. They argue that because the Jews crucified Jesus (though, as mentioned earlier on, the Gentiles also had their share in the crucifixion) the Christians are now called to punish the Jews, the latter having been rejected by God. But in His Word God clearly says that He has not rejected His people:

> Thus says the Lord: 'If the heavens above can be measured, and the foundations of the earth below

> can be explored, then I will cast off all the descen-
> dants of Israel for all that they have done.'
>
> Jeremiah 31:37; cf. 33:25f.; Hosea 11:8f.

According to Romans 11, the Lord will graft the people of Israel back into their own olive tree when His time has come. From Jeremiah 30:11 it is also evident that His people do not stand under final rejection but are undergoing chastening:

> Though I make a full end of all nations ... I will
> not make a complete end of you. But I will correct
> you in justice, and will not let you go altogether
> unpunished.   RAV

It is striving against the Word of God to say, 'God obviously must have intended the Jews to be exterminated. Otherwise He would not have given Hitler the liberty to wipe them out to such an extent.'

If only we had the eyes to see, we would realize that this heaviest of blows inflicted upon them by God was in fact expressive of His great love. Though the cost in tears and unspeakable suffering has been terrible, it was this stroke that has kept His chosen people from total assimilation with the so-called Christian nations, driving them back into the land of their fathers. The Jews otherwise would never have returned home in such great numbers. At every opportunity they would have settled down permanently in their host nations and become assimilated. The pioneer work to be done in the land of their fathers would probably have appeared to most of them as being too hard. It was the cruel trials of the worst years of persecution that drove them home.

Once long ago the Lord used the sin and guilt of Pharaoh to drive His people out of Egypt into Canaan. Today there has been another Pharaoh who has afflicted them in a far more terrible way till they left for the land of Canaan, which the Lord has allocated to them. There He would have His people dwell and nowhere else. The time of dispersion was always meant to be but a temporary period of judgment. God has not cast off His people for ever: He has only chastened them and visited them with the greatest of sufferings. He has led them back home to their land, and He is also leading them back to His heart.

'The gifts and the call of God are irrevocable.' His gifts to His people are, firstly, His land, the land of Canaan and, secondly, their continued posterity. This is why the people of Israel could not be exterminated. This is why a remnant had to remain, as the prophets have always foretold. The Jewish people cannot perish, though most of the nations of antiquity have perished, for the Lord intends to fulfil all His promises. And this is why we are currently witnessing a unique phase in divine history. Before our eyes the restoration of Israel is beginning to take place with the same precision as God's many judgments upon her.

The people of God have literally been scattered among all nations (Deuteronomy 4:27). They have literally been without king or prince, without sacrifice or ephod (Hosea 3:4). The nations have in fact considered them to be a 'byword of cursing' (Zechariah 8:13). But just as the curses have been fulfilled to the letter, so too will the promises of blessing be fulfilled, for everything that God says in His Word will come to pass, literally and precisely.

If we Christians have regarded in the past and still regard today all the Old Testament curses and judgments pronounced against His people as being only for Israel, must we not also view the promises to Israel of grace and blessing in the same way? Must we not take them literally, believing that these promises will be fulfilled for Israel as an earthly people, rather than spiritualizing them and appropriating them for us Christians? It would be illogical to regard all the judgments as applying to Israel, and all the promises of blessing to ourselves. Accordingly, such promises of blessing and renewed fruitfulness of the land of Israel cannot be interpreted as spiritual blessings for the people of the new covenant, but rather as a tangible reality for an earthly people, the people of Israel. If we Christians suddenly say that Scripture's promises of blessing — though not, please note, the judgments — are to be taken only spiritually, thus claiming them for ourselves, our interpretation of Scripture is dishonest and unacceptable. It has but one root: pride.

God, however, resists the proud. Only to the humble does He grant grace — the grace of seeing eyes, which recognize that God draws near not only to us but also to others, in this case to Israel. Such a humble attitude towards God's promises to Israel does not exclude the fact that as Christians we may also apply the Old Testament promises to our personal lives. Israel, however, is the actual recipient of the promises, in whom they will be fulfilled in their original and concrete sense, and this truth must remain incontestable.

But is it not so in every age that the pious and devout, those who think they are nearest to God, those who claim to see, are very often blind and least capable of discerning the ways of God and His dealings with man? Thus we in our piety, we who live by the Scriptures and refer to them, largely fail to comprehend the significance of this point in redemptive history when a new phase has begun in God's dealings with His chosen people.

Yet as a sign that this turning-point has come for Israel, God performs miracle after miracle, as for instance when the tiny Israeli army defeated the well-equipped armies of seven Arab states. President Ben-Zvi said at the ninth anniversary of the foundation of the state of Israel, 'We have again experienced a Hanukkah miracle equal to the one we celebrate year by year: "You have given over the strong to the weak; many were delivered up to the few." Pharaoh's chariots and horsemen were beaten and scattered to the four winds, routed by the Israel Defence Forces.'

Yes, God is performing miracles again, as He has promised:

> As in the days when you came out of Egypt, I will show them my wonders. Nations will see and be ashamed, deprived of all their power.
>
> Micah 7:15f. NIV

Often we fail to perceive God's miracles, just as Pharaoh repeatedly refused to recognize them, though they were performed before his eyes.

David Ben-Gurion says, 'Whoever does not believe in miracles is not a realist.' But we European Christians have been so blinded by our intellect, which has not been brought under the captivity of obedience to Christ, that mere intellectual objections render us incapable of believing.

When will we believe in a miracle? Where and when did we recognize the hand of God doing miracles in world events or in our personal lives? Are we not inclined to give a natural explanation to all occurrences? We need again to learn from our elder brother Israel that we have a God who performs miracles. Signs and wonders have always been associated with Israel, God's chosen people, and the same is true today, whereas among the nations few miracles are to be seen.

During the centuries of dispersion, the arm of God was withdrawn. But now, since the Jews have returned to their land and have once more become a nation, God shows the world again that He belongs to this people and proves by signs and wonders that He is leading them. Miracles happen even in the realm of nature. Since the beginning of the century (for the first time in 1902) the former and latter rains, which had ceased in the first centuries after Christ, in fulfilment of the word of judgment in Jeremiah 3:3, have recommenced. With this, the promise of blessing in Joel 2:23 has come to pass.

Through all these events God wants to open the eyes of us Christians, so that not only Israel but we too may recognize this crucial hour in redemptive history, clearly referred to in Romans 11.

If our hearts are attuned to Jesus, we shall recognize that hour, having awaited it together with Him. If we but realized how the Father-heart of God has waited in love and anguish these two thousand years until He could once more let His face shine upon His people; until He could withdraw His severest chastening, the dispersion among the nations; until He could console them by leading them back home to the land of their fathers. How He must have yearned for the time when the exiles would once again become a people with their own state! No longer despised and hated aliens, they could live there proudly and happily as free citizens. What joy for our Father in heaven that now, at last, His people can fully develop their manifold, God-given abilities in their own land, on their own soil — an opportunity denied them for centuries.

Chapter 12

God's Call to Sympathize and Rejoice with Israel

G OD'S HEART is full of joy. Should we not rejoice with Him? Should we not look upon Israel, God's special love, as God looks upon her now? Little by little His judgment is turning into grace. The dispersion is gradually being replaced by the homecoming of the Jews. The longing of two thousand years and the pain of being so far away from Jerusalem have for many come to an end. The land of the fathers is opened again for Israel; she has re-entered the Promised Land. Should not this great moment cause a stir within Christendom as it must do in the heavenly places where Israel's return is eagerly watched? The prophets must be rejoicing at this moment for which they have waited thousands of years, the moment when their prophecies concerning Israel's restoration are beginning to be fulfilled! Certainly no Christian can remain indifferent to this event.

Are we not filled with joy that Israel's restoration has now begun and that she has returned to her own country? Do our hearts not thrill with gladness at the sight of arid terrain being changed into a garden, and ruined cities being rebuilt, as God repeatedly promised thousands of years ago as a token of special grace and glory? Indeed, for two thousand years, this land was literally a wilderness — without water, without trees, without gardens or cultivated ground. Wherever the eye looked there was nothing but stones to be seen, with only an occasional town. But today, before our very eyes, the prophecy has become reality:

> I am the Lord ... who confirms the word of his servant, and performs the counsel of his messengers; who says of Jerusalem, 'She shall be inhabited,' and of the cities of Judah, 'They shall be built, and I will raise up their ruins.'   Isaiah 44:24,26

Within a few years of the foundation of the state hundreds of new settlements came into existence, many of them with names taken from Holy Scripture.

Yes, today we can drive on a well-built road through the Negev Desert to the Dead Sea, as the Lord has said:

> I will make a way in the wilderness and rivers in the desert.   Isaiah 43:19

As a matter of fact, water pipelines have been laid through the desert. Before our eyes, green trees are growing in the wilderness, in fulfilment of Scripture:

> I will put in the wilderness the cedar, the acacia, the myrtle, and the olive; I will set in the desert the cypress, the plane and the pine together.
> Isaiah 41:19

Why does the Lord do this? He adds, by way of answer,

> That men may see and know, may consider and understand together, that the hand of the Lord has done this, the Holy One of Israel has created it.
>
> Isaiah 41:20

Oh, do we take this to heart, and do we see in all this the hand of God, or do we try to give a natural explanation for all that is taking place in Israel? God repeatedly says that He inspires prophecies of future events in order that, when they come to pass, people will have to acknowledge that the fulfilment comes from Him, and that it is He who has predicted them. Considering all that is now happening in Israel, we can only worship God, who in His love is about to bring His eternal purposes to completion, as we can see with our own eyes. Yes,

> the people who survive the sword will find favour in the desert; I will come to give rest to Israel . . . I will build you up again and you will be rebuilt, O Virgin Israel. Again you will take up your tambourines and go out to dance with the joyful.
>
> Jeremiah 31:2,4 NIV

And today Israel's young people can be seen dancing at harvest time and on feast days, not modern steps but folk dances, many of which are based on Bible texts.

It is a moving experience to see this people back in their own country, working in their gardens, as the Lord has said:

> Again you shall plant vineyards upon the mountains of Samaria; the planters shall plant, and shall enjoy the fruit.　　　　　　　　Jeremiah 31:5

The Word of God is indeed Yea and Amen, and a highly significant moment has come in divine history as promises, thousands of years old, now begin to be fulfilled. Seeing all these things come to pass, are we not filled with praise and wonder?

> Rejoice with Jerusalem; be glad with her, all you who love her, you who mourned for her.
>
> Isaiah 66:10 LB

What a privilege to love Israel, to express that love in action, and to offer her sacrificial gifts! Let us avail ourselves wholeheartedly of this privilege and, as co-workers with God, serve Him by helping the people of Israel develop their country and turn the desert into a garden of Eden so that they may soon enjoy its fruits and, moreover, soon be transformed themselves and filled with the glory of God!

But what tremendous opportunities we can miss if we stand aloof from this mighty working of God, if we remain uninvolved, if we do not permit Him to kindle a love for Israel in us! When the Lord comes again to establish His kingdom, we may then find ourselves excluded. So now, as Israel begins to develop her land and national life, as she fights for her very existence, may we share her burdens and cares, for this is the Lord's command to us in view of His people's homecoming:

> Go through, go through the gates, prepare the way for the people; build up, build up the highway, clear it of stones.
>
> Isaiah 62:10

Yes, it is the hour of return, of the great homecoming! The Lord bids us rejoice because He has drawn near to Israel again.

> Thus says the Lord: 'Sing aloud with gladness for Jacob, and raise shouts for the chief of the nations; proclaim, give praise, and say, "The Lord has saved his people, the remnant of Israel." Behold, I will bring them from the north country, and gather them from the farthest parts of the earth . . . a great company, they shall return here.'   Jeremiah 31:7f.

Furthermore, the Lord challenges us:

> Hear the word of the Lord, O nations, and declare it in the coastlands afar off; say, 'He who scattered Israel will gather him, and will keep him as a shepherd keeps his flock.'   Jeremiah 31:10

This message really deserves to be universally proclaimed because it magnifies the glory of God, who so wonderfully fulfils His ancient promises. What we read in Isaiah 43:5f. is now coming true:

> Fear not, for I am with you; I will bring your offspring from the east, and from the west I will gather you; I will say to the north, Give up, and to the south, Do not withhold; bring my sons from afar and my daughters from the end of the earth.

The time has now come when

> it shall no longer be said, 'As the Lord lives who brought up the people of Israel out of the land of Egypt,' but 'As the Lord lives who brought up the people of Israel out of the north country and out of all the countries where he had driven them.' For I will bring them back to their own land which I gave to their fathers.   Jeremiah 16:14f.

No other return from previous captivities in the history of this people is to be compared with this return which has now begun. The return from the captivity in Babylon (538 BC) was only the initial stage of the fulfilment of the prophecies. It was only a partial fulfilment. About fifty thousand of the tribe of Judah and Benjamin returned from Babylon, and only from that one country (Ezra 2). But the prophetic Word speaks of the return of the Jews of all twelve tribes (Jeremiah 3:18; 30:3; 31:1; 33:7; 50:4; Ezekiel 37:15ff.; Hosea 1:11; Zechariah 10:6). They will return from all nations and countries (Zechariah 8:7; Isaiah 11:10ff.; Jeremiah 16:14f.; 31:2; 31:8; Ezekiel 11:16f.; 36:24).

The Jews who returned from Babylon, and their descendants, remained in the land of Canaan a relatively short time, but the return from all countries and peoples announced by the prophets is declared to be a permanent one. Amos writes about it (ch. 9:15). And it is written in Jeremiah,

> My eyes will watch over them for their good, and I will bring them back to this land. I will build them up and not tear them down; I will plant them and not uproot them. Jeremiah 24:6 NIV

Furthermore, the Prophet Zechariah prophesies ca. 518 BC, namely, after the return from Babylon, of a future return of the Jews from the nations into the land of their fathers (Zechariah 8:7f.). And the Prophet Isaiah says,

> In that day the Lord will extend his hand yet a second time to recover the remnant which is left of his people, from Assyria, from Egypt, from Pathros, from Ethiopia, from Elam, from Shinar, from Hamath, and from the coastlands of the sea. Isaiah 11:11

This hour has now arrived. Should we not, therefore, sing aloud with gladness and make it known in the farthest corners of the earth? This is our task today if we are concerned for the honour of God's name.

A highly significant moment has come in divine history. Once again God has ushered in the age of miracles and mighty deeds among His people Israel. Woe to him who, instead of rejoicing at the graciousness of God, now causes hurt to the apple of God's eye. Israel is holy to the Lord.

The time has come, of which it is said, 'Comfort, comfort my people.' If a woe was pronounced against those who were the instruments of judgment upon Israel in the past, particularly those who carried it out with so much cruelty, do not those also deserve divine judgment — those who oppose Israel at the present time when God has again looked favourably on His people and restored them to their own country? Then the scripture will come to pass:

> Whoever stirs up strife with you shall fall because of you.   Isaiah 54:15

Blessed, however, are those who wish Israel well today, for the Scriptures say of such, 'They shall prosper that love thee' (Psalm 122:6 AV). Blessed is he who respects this people as the special possession of God, of the living, eternal God, the Most High, and acknowledges that Israel is His first-born son, His darling child, the very apple of His eye. Blessed is he who meets this people with reverence because they are the chosen people of God; blessed is he who fears to do them harm or to injure them in any way. Blessed is the nation and the man that do good to Israel. Such acts bring joy to the heart of God, which overflows with love for His people.

Chapter 13

The Second Phase in the New Era

IF THE HOUR of Israel's return marks the dawning of her restoration, her regained nationhood
is a sign that the second promise too will soon be
fulfilled. After the dry bones have come together,
life and spirit will enter them. The Prophet Ezekiel
prophesies not only that God will open the graves
and cause His people to come up from their
'graves' — that is, the countries of their dispersion
— and bring them home to the land of Israel
(Ezekiel 37:12). No, he prophesies even more.

This brings us to the second phase towards
which Israel is now moving. For as surely as
Ezekiel's first prophecy is being fulfilled, so also
will the second be fulfilled:

> Prophesy to the breath, prophesy, son of man, and
> say to the breath, Thus says the Lord God: Come
> from the four winds, O breath, and breathe upon
> these slain, that they may live.   Ezekiel 37:9

> I will put my Spirit within you, and you shall live.
>   Ezekiel 37:14

When Ezekiel, after his first prophecy, became
aware of a rattling sound as the dry bones came
together, he saw that there were sinews and flesh

upon them, overlaid with skin, but the breath of life was not yet in them. Then Ezekiel was again permitted to utter a prophecy, a message to the Spirit of Life: 'Come...O breath, and breathe upon these slain, that they may live.' And, behold, they were imbued with life.

Great and mighty things lie in store for Israel. God is not satisfied with bringing His people back from the ends of the earth to re-establish them in their land, thus reassembling the dry bones. No, God is the God of the living, and He, the living God, desires that His people may be filled with divine life. He desires the Spirit to enter them — the Spirit who awakens repentance, the Spirit who kindles love for God in people's hearts and unites them again with the living God. May we not assume that this prophecy is linked with the coming of the Messiah? The Messiah will be able to reveal Himself to His people when they are filled with longing for Him. God reveals Himself to those who wait for Him. He draws near to the humble and penitent. These are the ones He visits. As it is written in Isaiah 57:15, God, the high and lofty One, dwells with those that are of a contrite and humble heart. And the Prophet Malachi says that, before the great and terrible day of the Lord comes, another Elijah, a preacher of repentance, will first appear.

When the Spirit of God descends upon Israel, this will no doubt be accompanied by a fresh outpouring of repentance. We read in Holy Scripture, 'Sanctify yourselves; for tomorrow the Lord will do wonders among you' (Joshua 3:5). Whenever the Lord approached His people, be it on Sinai or in order to perform a miracle, He commanded them beforehand to cleanse themselves, to make a break with sin and to repent.

This time the coming of the Spirit will be so powerful that it will sweep like a mighty wind upon all Israel, making their hearts quail before the holy God, as they come to recognize the depth of man's sinfulness. Then they will see the King in His beauty, and, as the Prophet Jeremiah foretold, God will put His law within them, writing it upon their hearts, so that

> no longer shall each man teach his neighbour and each his brother, saying, 'Know the Lord,' for they shall all know me, from the least of them to the greatest ... for I will forgive their iniquity, and I will remember their sin no more.   Jeremiah 31:34

When repentance begins to break out and God can forgive the sins of those who come to Him filled with contrition, He will reveal Himself. Then the Messiah will be seen and the day of salvation will dawn.

For the people of Israel this now entails living in expectation of this day and praying that God will deal with them in accordance with Ezekiel's prophecy. It is a matter of them yielding themselves completely to God and giving Him the right response to all His paths of chastening and judgment, to all the sufferings and afflictions that the returned people have still to endure, especially in the time of the Antichrist. And that is the response made by Job: 'I ... abhor myself, and repent in dust and ashes' (Job 42:6 AB). Then judgment will be turned into grace, which will be poured out abundantly upon God's people.

Compared with the second phase, the first phase — Israel's physical return — will appear insignificant. So tremendous will this second phase be that it will be analogous to a resurrection from the dead. Israel will be filled with the divine breath of life from Him who created her, to whom she belongs, to whom she is bound for ever, and she will be restored to her eternal destiny. Indeed, what are we human beings without the divine breath of life within us? Then redeemed Israel will shine forth with perfect beauty. Then it will become manifest that Israel bears in herself the glory of God.

Because this hour has drawn near, we Christians ought to sing to Israel in our hearts and with our tongues the song of her glory, the song of her election, consecration and calling. For the truth is that Israel is called by God; she will be made glorious; she will shine in the beauty of God; she will be the centre of all nations and the blessing for all peoples. Indeed,

> out of Zion shall go forth the law, and the word of
> the Lord from Jerusalem.   Isaiah 2:3

To this Zion-Jerusalem it has been promised that, in the latter days, peoples and nations will come flowing to her, saying,

> Come, let us go up to the mountain of the Lord, to
> the house of the God of Jacob; that he may teach
> us his ways and we may walk in his paths.
>   Micah 4:2

Thus Israel will be a blessing for the nations:

> Many peoples and strong nations shall come to
> seek the Lord of hosts in Jerusalem, and to entreat
> the favour of the Lord . . . In those days ten men
> from the nations of every tongue shall take hold of
> the robe of a Jew, saying, 'Let us go with you, for
> we have heard that God is with you.'
>
> Zechariah 8:22f.

PART THREE

*God's Loving Dealings
with Israel*

Chapter 14

God Prepares His People

WHOEVER WANTS to come to know the heart of God will do so by acquainting himself with His people Israel. Let him consider God's leadings for His people. From an earthly father's dealings with his son we are given a glimpse of his deepest relationship to his child, so too from God's dealings with Israel, His first-born son. We can learn from God's leadings for Israel His attitude towards the sons of men in general and what purposes are in His heart when He leads us one way or the other, along paths of judgment or paths of grace. For we read of both in the history of Israel.

Indeed, Israel, as the beloved child of God, is set before us as a mirror reflecting the heart of God, showing us who God is. We see that He is the Father of love, for only a loving heart can pour abundant grace over a people and prepare glory for them, such as we see prepared for the people of Israel. Only a loving heart can break out in lamentation when its love is unrequited or when the beloved follows paths of sin, which lead to ruin. However dearly an earthly father may love his child, he could never grieve over him the way God grieves over His people, as expressed in the words of Holy Scripture. This is not to be taken merely as a proof that Israel has sinned a great deal and was a wicked people. Admittedly, Israel did sin a great deal and engaged in many evil practices. But the fact that God grieves and laments so deeply is primarily indicative of His loving heart.

In His love God has set His heart on this tiny nation, as it is written:

> For the vineyard of the Lord of hosts is the house of Israel, and the men of Judah are his pleasant planting.   Isaiah 5:7

In another place God speaks of Israel as being precious to Him. Because He loves her, He declares that He will give nations as a ransom for her, and peoples in exchange for her life (Isaiah 43:3f.). For the very reason that God loves His people so dearly, it grieves Him deeply when He sees that Israel does not bear His likeness, that she is not a holy nation unto Him, but that she walks in evil ways:

> I planted you a choice vine, wholly of pure seed. How then have you turned degenerate and become a wild vine?   Jeremiah 2:21

It is very moving to hear the laments pouring from the Father-heart of God as He grieves over His people:

> I thought you would call me, My Father, and would not turn from following me. Surely, as a faithless wife leaves her husband, so have you been faithless to me, O house of Israel.
>   Jeremiah 3:19f.

And:

> Can a maiden forget her ornaments, or a bride her attire? Yet my people have forgotten me days without number.
>
> Jeremiah 2:32

> Have you seen what she did, that faithless one, Israel, how she went up on every high hill and under every green tree, and there played the harlot? And I thought, 'After she has done all this she will return to me'; but she did not return.
>
> Jeremiah 3:6f.

> O Israel, my sinful people, come home to me again, for I am merciful; I will not be forever angry with you. Only acknowledge your guilt; admit that you rebelled against the Lord your God and committed adultery against him.
>
> Jeremiah 3:12f. LB

We also read:

> Has a nation ever changed its gods? (Yet they are not gods at all.) But my people have exchanged their Glory for worthless idols. Be appalled at this, O heavens, and shudder with great horror.
>
> Jeremiah 2:11 NIV

> What fault did your fathers find in me, that they strayed so far from me? They followed worthless idols and became worthless themselves. They did not ask, 'Where is the Lord, who brought us up out of Egypt?'
>
> Jeremiah 2:5f. NIV

> Perhaps they will listen [to what the prophet says] and each will turn from his evil way. Then I will relent and not bring on them the disaster I was planning because of the evil they have done.
>
> Jeremiah 26:3 NIV

Such is the lament of God, the Father of Israel. But amid the lamentations over the sin of His people, the mercy of God breaks through like the sun between the clouds and He says:

> I have seen his ways, but I will heal him; I will
> guide him and restore comfort to him, creating
> praise on the lips of the mourners in Israel.
>
> > Isaiah 57:18f. NIV

> For I will not contend for ever, neither will I be
> angry always, for [were it not so] the spirit [of
> man] would faint and be consumed before Me,
> and [My purpose in] creating the souls of men
> would be frustrated. Isaiah 57:16 AB

Precisely when Israel has grieved God with her
many sins, forcing Him to pronounce judgment,
He repeatedly breaks off to plead with His people.
He speaks not as a remote God, who does nothing
but utter judgment, but as a Father, whose loving
heart goes out to His people and who grieves
when He is obliged to chasten them, a sentiment
reflected in such passages as the following:

> How can I give you up, O Ephraim! How can I
> hand you over, O Israel! How can I make you like
> Admah! How can I treat you like Zeboiim [Admah
> and Zeboiim were cities of the plain, destroyed
> along with Sodom]! My heart recoils within me,
> my compassion grows warm and tender.
>
> > Hosea 11:8

It is deeply moving to find again and again in
the prophetic writings that the Lord pauses amid
His proclamations of judgment and, as it were,
speaks to Himself, scarcely able to bring Himself
to punish His people, even though He is obliged
to, if He loves them, in order to set them right. But
He cannot do so without His compassion growing
'warm and tender'. So dear to Him is His child
Israel (Jeremiah 31:20) that as often as He speaks
against him He remembers him in His mercy.

Where else are we given such a glimpse into the heart of God as here in His dealings with Israel — into this living heart, which is angry with His people and which in the midst of wrath pauses and once again offers grace? Even while executing judgment, He is overcome with compassion, so that He is compelled to refresh and comfort His people who, like all of us, have deserved nothing but His wrath. Thus we read in Isaiah 51:3,

> For the Lord will comfort Zion; he will comfort all her waste places.

And in Zechariah 10:6,

> I have compassion on them, and they shall be as though I had not rejected them.

Still another example of the compassionate heart of God can be found in Amos 7:2f., where in answer to the prayer of Amos He reduced the severity of judgment:

> When they [the locusts] had finished eating the grass of the land, I said, 'O Lord God, forgive, I beseech thee! How can Jacob stand? He is so small!' The Lord repented concerning this; 'It shall not be,' said the Lord.

At such dealings of God we can only exclaim with the Prophet Micah:

> Who is a God like thee, pardoning iniquity and passing over transgression for the remnant of his inheritance? He does not retain his anger for ever because he delights in steadfast love.   Micah 7:18

From all of God's dealings with Israel we can see that His heart rejoices in showing mercy and kindness, in making His people happy, in pouring out abundant blessings upon them for body, soul and spirit, and in filling them with His glory. Even the severe judgments that befell them, their dire, centuries-long afflictions and the dark pathways they had to follow, need to be seen in this light. Behind it all was the overflowing love of God, whose one desire is to show grace, even if He first has to pave the way by sending judgment.

Only with this in mind can we understand the fierce wrath of God, which breaks forth in the divinely inspired utterances of the prophets. It is the wrath of the thrice holy God which often fills people with such dread that they deny that He is a God of Love and a Father. If He were Love, they say, He would never have allowed, for instance, the atrocities of the concentration camps.

The wrath of God and the terror of His judgments, however, can be rightly understood only if we know the loving heart of God. A father grows angry only when his loving requests and exhortations are of no avail. Only when he has no other choice does he resort to methods that are a grief to him. The child is so obstinate, his heart so hardened, that nothing else will induce him to turn from his sinful ways. In the face of such stubbornness, a father's wrath is an expression of his desperate love as he seeks to win back his child from paths of evil. And even if a father has to send away his child, to the child's great distress, and put him in a reform school for many years, again he is prompted only by love, since there is no other way of helping his child, who is bent on a course that spells ruin for himself.

Yes, the wrath of God is an anguished wrath, from which we can see how greatly we have provoked and grieved Him and how great our sin is, so that He says, 'You have burdened me with your sins, you have wearied me with your iniquities' (Isaiah 43:24). That God should manifest His wrath to such an extent reveals how much He loves us and how great is the divine jealousy He feels for us. He will go to any lengths to draw us out of the quicksand of sin, because sin is our ruin. Thus He spares us no blows, although they cost Him untold pain, as is indicated time and again by His laments in the books of the prophets.

Nowhere can we see so clearly the holiness and power of the divine wrath as in God's dealings with His people Israel. Unlike human actions, all of God's actions are characterized by authority, strength and majesty. We know of human father-love, but this is infinitesimal compared with the fiery love characteristic of the Father-heart of God. We know of a father's anger, and yet it too is but a tiny spark compared with the blazing intensity of God's holy wrath, which is poured out upon His people and which, at the end of world history, will be poured out upon all mankind. Time and again God has held back His wrath and waited in patience, adding yet another year of grace, because His loving heart could not bear to send judgment. But when all else has failed and iniquity comes to a peak, then judgment, long deferred, can be restrained no longer; with unparalleled force it breaks out against a people and, at the end of time, it will break out against the whole human race.

Why? In order that souls might still be saved. Again, this is evident in the case of Israel. But why with her more than with other peoples? The reason is that Israel, as His first-born, is the special object of His love. At all costs He wants to transform her and fill her with His glory in accordance with her calling: 'You shall be to me...a holy nation' (Exodus 19:6).

If Israel was to attain her exalted calling to be a blessing for all nations, God was obliged to prepare her by leading her along paths of severe chastening and by not refraining from this greatest expression of His love: His holy wrath.

This has already begun to bear fruit. After the horrors of the extermination camps, Israel at last started to return home on a massive scale. During World War II, a similar thing happened to Christians who had fallen away from the Lord. After being afflicted by God with wartime hardships and detention in prison camp, many of them regained their faith and have come back to their heavenly Father.

Could we but once see the fruit of divine visitations, we would praise and worship God for sparing neither Himself nor us in taking us along those paths that ultimately lead to our well-being, salvation and happiness. This, rather than an indulgent love, is true love and serves our highest good.

Let us not always measure God according to our standards and think of Him in terms of our human concepts. Certainly, all that is of this world is a shadow of the real thing, as, for instance, human fatherhood. Nevertheless, God is unique. His love cannot be compared to human love; nor can His holy, awesome wrath be likened to human anger.

> At the noise of the tumult [caused by Your voice at which the enemy is overthrown] the peoples flee; at the lifting up of Yourself nations are scattered. Isaiah 33:3 AB

> Men will flee to caves in the rocks and to holes in the ground from dread of the Lord and the splendour of his majesty, when he rises to shake the earth. Isaiah 2:19 NIV

> Who of us can dwell with the consuming fire? Who of us can dwell with everlasting burning? Isaiah 33:14 NIV

> At his wrath the earth quakes, and the nations cannot endure his indignation. Jeremiah 10:10

This is the wrathful God, whose wrath Israel has experienced more than any other people. To the extent that God loved and continues to love His people, to that extent they had to taste His wrath, so that they would not be cast off for ever but be led back to Him and attain their glorious destiny.

Oh, if only we would always see the judgments of God against the backdrop of His love! Holy Scripture is full of warnings of divine judgment for Israel, but if we were to compare them with God's promises of grace for her, we would discover that grace outweighs judgment and that judgment is meant to bring forth grace. Because God is Love, He yearns to receive our love. We show that His love has awakened a response in us if we comply with His wishes, accept His will and obey His commandments, and if we do not oppose Him even when we do not understand His painful visitations.

Israel gave her response of love to God under inconceivably bitter sufferings. Even in the horrors of the Warsaw Ghetto, when set upon by dogs, doomed to starvation and on the verge of despair, she proved her devotion; her song of faith could not be silenced:

> *I believe, I believe, I believe*
> *Sincerely, firmly and devoutly*
> *In the coming of the Messiah.*
>
> *I believe in the Messiah*
> *And, though He tarry,*
> *No less firmly, I believe.*
>
> *And though He tarry longer still,*
> *Nevertheless, I believe in the Messiah.*
> *I believe, I believe, I believe.*

Song of the ghetto martyrs

Chapter 15

Suffering Changed to Glory

THE HISTORY of the people of Israel is marked by disgrace, persecution, humiliation, ostracism, poverty and severe affliction. But it does not end there. With God, suffering can end only in glory: the humiliated will be exalted and the glory of God will rise upon them; the despised will be honoured by all. This is a law of Holy Scripture. We read, for instance, in the Book of Isaiah,

> O afflicted one, storm-tossed, and not comforted, behold, I will set your stones in antimony, and lay your foundations with sapphires.   Isaiah 54:11

And in the Sermon on the Mount:

> Blessed are those who mourn, for they shall be comforted.   Matthew 5:4

> Blessed are those who are persecuted for righteousness' sake, for theirs is the kingdom of heaven.
> Matthew 5:10

> Blessed are you that hunger now, for you shall be satisfied. Blessed are you that weep now, for you shall laugh. Blessed are you when men hate you, and when they exclude you and revile you, and cast out your name as evil, on account of the Son of man! Rejoice in that day, and leap for joy, for behold, your reward is great in heaven.   Luke 6:21ff.

The latter is a promise especially for those who suffer on account of God, and so it is also a promise for His people Israel. Indeed, they have suffered for the very reason that they are God's chosen people, apart from the fact that they have also suffered for their sins. Christians, too, are led along paths of disgrace, humiliation, ostracism and affliction on account of their sins as well as on God's account.

Because God is so merciful, because He is so loving, He has pity on everyone who has to undergo suffering. He does not say, 'This is only right. You are a sinner. As a punishment for your sins you have to follow these paths and suffer humiliation, disgrace and sorrow!' No, because His heart grieves with us when we suffer, He cannot but take us in His embrace at the end of our paths of suffering and comfort us as a true father. Thus after the severe trials of His people He makes this appeal on their behalf:

> Comfort my people ... Comfort them ... Tell them they have suffered long enough and their sins are now forgiven. I have punished them in full for all their sins.   Isaiah 40:1f. GNB

After times of suffering because of our sins, consolation awaits us. When guilt has been atoned for through the judgment endured (Isaiah 27:8f.), there will be gladness and rejoicing instead of sorrow. As the God of Love, our Father cannot bear to see a person's life filled with nothing but sorrow. With God suffering is never the final outcome. Love makes every effort to bring happiness to others. If this is true of us human beings, how much more so of God, who is the very essence of love and fatherhood!

The sorely afflicted people of Israel, bleeding from many wounds, will find that their path of sorrows ends in glory. They will shine forth in beauty and gladness, and the radiant splendour of the Lord will rest upon this people — the glory accorded to those held in great contempt. Then the saying will be fulfilled:

> Nations shall come to your light, and kings to the brightness of your rising. Isaiah 60:3

A flood of light will emanate from this people, shining far and wide into the world, so that the nations are attracted by it. They will be dazzled by the splendour of Israel.

Just as once people expressed all their contempt in the word 'Jew', using it as a term of abuse; just as they were unwilling to be associated with Jews; so now their attitude will be exactly the opposite. The words 'Jew' and 'people of Israel' will be pronounced, no longer as an insult, but with the greatest reverence as a blessing and a greeting. Instead of shunning Jews, people will seek them out.

This will be true of the new generation, which has experienced nothing of the past Jew-hatred and contempt, but even more so of those who at every turn had despised, oppressed and insulted the Jews. All these will draw near. Whole nations will enter the gates of Jerusalem and, as the Lord says in Isaiah 60:14, 'all who despised you shall bow down at your feet'. They will then confess openly that Jerusalem and its inhabitants, the Jews, are 'the City of the Lord, the Zion of the Holy One of Israel'. They will be lost in wonder and praise, because they can see that here is a people among whom the living God has made His abode. He who is their Maker too has revealed Himself here, endowing this people with His glory. For centuries the Jews have been hated and neglected; they were unvisited in their ghettos; they were shunned when forced to wear the yellow star of shame; but now the promise of Isaiah 60:15 will come to pass. This people will be made the 'everlasting pride' (NIV), so that everyone will be proud of being associated with a Jew or the people of Israel.

Yes, this people will be the 'joy of all generations' (NIV). Only wonderful things will be told of this people, of their city and its life, how all is transfused with divine glory, and how the Messiah Himself reigns there. They will be praised as a righteous people (Isaiah 60:21), a kingdom governed, as no other kingdom on earth, with justice according to wonderful, divine laws; a kingdom of happiness and well-being. All nations that know Israel will have to acknowledge that they are a people whom the Lord has blessed (Isaiah 61:9). The splendour of the glory that will radiate from the city of Jerusalem and the entire people of Israel is beyond imagination. Isaiah prophetically describes it:

> ... her righteousness goes forth as brightness, and her salvation as a lamp that burns. The Gentiles shall see your righteousness.　　Isaiah 62:1f. RAV

This people will have a special dignity and distinction. In their judgments they will exercise justice. They will be the very soul of integrity, and their faces will reflect the beauty of God. All their actions will be marked by benevolence and love. They will outshine all other nations because divine favour will rest upon them. In recompense for all the abusive names attached to them, this people will receive a new name, which, as is written in Isaiah 62:2, 'the mouth of the Lord will give' and which all nations will pronounce with reverence. The formerly despised Jews will be referred to as 'The holy people' and 'Hephzibah', signifying 'My delight is in her'; and instead of being called 'Forsaken', Jerusalem will now be called 'Sought out, a city not forsaken' (Isaiah 62:4,12).

Jerusalem will be made 'a praise in the earth' (Isaiah 62:7). Israel will be renowned among all the nations, and just as she was hated and scorned, she will now be loved and highly honoured. It is overwhelming to see how the Lord recompenses His people's times of shame and ostracism in double measure, as is written:

> Instead of your shame you shall have a double portion, instead of dishonour you shall rejoice in your lot. Isaiah 61:7

Indeed, 'Israel shall blossom and put forth shoots, and fill the whole world with fruit' (Isaiah 27:6), fruit of the intellect, wisdom and knowledge in the realm of art and science. And the words will come true:

> Kings shall see and arise; princes, and they shall prostrate themselves; because of the Lord, who is

> faithful, the Holy One of Israel, who has chosen
> you.   Isaiah 49:7

There among this people He will make His abode.
There the nations will seek Him, as Scripture says:

> Many peoples and strong nations shall come to
> seek the Lord of hosts in Jerusalem, and to entreat
> the favour of the Lord.   Zechariah 8:22

There are countless passages in the Scriptures
where the Lord speaks of the future glory of His
people. It is as if He cannot give enough assur-
ances to His people who, having lived in shame
and ignominy for two thousand years, probably
find it hard to believe that this time will come. It
is as if He cannot impress upon them enough that
they will yet be exalted:

> I will change their shame into praise and renown
> in all the earth.   Zephaniah 3:19

Further, He says,

> At that time I will bring you home, at the time
> when I gather you together; yea, I will make you
> renowned and praised among all the peoples of
> the earth, when I restore your fortunes before your
> eyes.   Zephaniah 3:20

This the Lord has promised.

And now in our times the great transformation
is beginning. Events move slowly and impercep-
tibly, because a great deal of the old contempt for
Israel still remains. Yet here and there in the
nations a new respect is emerging for this tiny
nation of Israel. Almost overnight the Jews have
established a national state in the land of their
fathers and are so courageously and devotedly

building up their country in the face of many enemies. But true recognition cannot come until Israel is under the rule of her Messiah. When that happens she will be universally acknowledged as once before in her early history:

> Your renown went forth among the nations because of your beauty, for it was perfect through the splendour which I had bestowed upon you.
> Ezekiel 16:14

Words cannot adequately express what it will be like when God invests His people with His beauty in the Messianic kingdom and when everything in this people that does not yet reflect His image is transformed and shines forth in incomparable splendour. It will be a fulfilment of the prophecies:

> The Lord, your God ... will rejoice over you with gladness, he will renew you in his love; he will exult over you with loud singing.   Zephaniah 3:17

> As the bridegroom rejoices over the bride, so shall your God rejoice over you.   Isaiah 62:5

— over this, His chosen and beloved people. All the promises made concerning this land will then be fulfilled, though at present it is still the centre of conflict and divided by barbed wire. It will be the land where God Himself will dwell, as is written in Zechariah 2:11 —

> I will dwell in the midst of you.

Everything that He has said will come to pass:

> I will return to Zion, and will dwell in the midst of Jerusalem, and Jerusalem shall be called the faithful city.   Zechariah 8:3

The Lord, your God, is in your midst.

Zephaniah 3:17

Out of Zion, the perfection of beauty, God shines forth.

Psalm 50:2

Yes, this is the secret of the beauty of this people and her land. This is the secret of her divine calling, which will reach its consummation when the Messiah, her King, dwells and rules in her midst. The counsels of God are truly wonderful and He fulfils them gloriously: through darkness to light, through chastenings and paths of judgment to supreme grace.

A Personal Testimony

Excerpts from the chapter 'God's People Israel' in Mother Basilea's autobiography, *A Foretaste of Heaven* (American edition: *I Found the Key to the Heart of God*)

Shortly before Christmas [1954] ... the Holy Spirit showed me God's suffering because of His chosen people. Today, just as in the past, Israel is a people especially loved by God. Referring to Israel, Scripture says, 'The gifts and the call of God are irrevocable' (Romans 11:29). Israel's long history of severe trials and afflictions testifies to this election ... But as a nation Israel has not yet turned to God and responded to His love, since she has not yet recognized her Messiah Jesus, although He came to her and laid down His life for her.

Whoever loves Jesus cannot bear to see Him wait in vain for the love of His people. This waiting, which is part of His sufferings today, filled me with distress and drove me to prayer. We have a custom of bringing God our special requests for the coming year at Christmas, since that is the festival when the Father manifests His loving goodness and blessings ... The Holy Spirit laid two requests upon my heart as the most urgent ones: 'Awaken souls amongst Your chosen people Israel to love You like a bride so that one day they may be with You in the City of God, upon whose gates the names of the twelve tribes of Israel are written [Revelation 21:12]. And please — a visit to Israel.'

My first wish was an expression of that which the Lord had laid upon my heart: His grief that not only had His people failed to receive Him two thousand years ago, but to this very day Israel has not yet found her way back to her Messiah. My second wish, however, came from the realization that as Christians we are also at fault — especially those of us from Germany — if His people cannot perceive the love of Jesus. Instead of showing special love and deference to God's chosen people, our nation committed unspeakable atrocities against them...

In my heart a deep feeling of contrition broke out, because in the hour of greatest distress for God's people I had taken too little trouble to show love to my Jewish brothers. Full of grief I could only cry from the depths of my heart, 'How can we heal the wounds that we have inflicted? How — if it is at all possible — can we make amends?'

During a week of prayer and fasting I was led by the Lord into deep intercession for Israel. In the creative power of His Spirit, who calls into existence the things that do not exist, God awakened in my heart a powerful love for Israel, His chosen people. Indeed, God's plan of salvation for Israel had always been important to me and I had openly held lectures on this topic throughout Germany even in the years from 1939 to 1944 despite the great risks involved. But this time a greater, more fervent love was granted to me. With this event God's Holy Spirit gave me a commission that was to involve the whole sisterhood — the Israel commission. During the talks I gave to my daughters about this new ministry in February 1955, repentance broke out amongst them — most of them had lived through the Third Reich as children or teenagers. As a small token of our contrition, for the following fifteen years while we were only German sisters, we stood in silence during breakfast in memory of the crime of our nation against Israel and of the millions in concentration camp who stood at roll-call. We used this time to bless Israel in our prayers. Today, since we have many sisters from other countries, we hold this prayer for Israel in a different way.

By granting us repentance, the Lord changed our attitude. No longer did we try to avoid the houses in our town where Jews lived, because we felt ashamed of the crime of our people; instead, we began to pay calls on them. Our first attempts at visiting Jewish people were met with marked reserve — a reaction which was understandable in view of the past. But in His grace God granted us a sign of His forgiveness; not only were we received in Jewish homes, but ever since then we have had the privilege of welcoming Jewish visitors from all over the world. The entire sisterhood was inspired with this love for Israel and from that time on Israel has played an important role in our life. Her sorrows and joys are ours as well.

Now the spiritual experiences I had ... were to materialize and to have outward effects. God granted my prayer for a journey to Israel. I scarcely trusted my eyes when I read the postmark on a letter that was slipped under my door one day. It was from Israel and contained an invitation. In those days it was necessary for a German to have an invitation from Israel in order to apply for a visa, although this was no guarantee that a visa would be granted. Until then few Germans had the opportunity of visiting this country, but without any complications Mother Martyria and I received the necessary papers — God's confirmation for the journey. Also, quite unexpectedly, we received a gift of money to cover the travelling expenses. The way seemed paved for us to go there in the autumn of 1955. But eight weeks before departure I fell seriously ill; my life was in danger. This was to be a time of preparation for my commission. Since the visit was to have far-reaching significance, it had to be underlaid with suffering. Then by the Lord's grace I recovered sufficiently to make the journey, and step by step we discovered that the Lord Himself had planned it and made all the preparations.

It was an indescribable moment when I first set foot upon the soil of the Holy Land, the ground trodden by Jesus, the Son of God. There I was to come to know His people, who had returned home from many nations, and to learn about their way of life in Israel. I was to meet His people, whom I had come to love so dearly.

When I arrived in Israel, I was still quite weak physically. Moreover, on the second day I stumbled, spraining my ankle so that I could scarcely walk. Had the Lord led me there only to confine me to bed for the duration of my stay? On the contrary, God used this accident to lead me throughout the land within a few short weeks. He had selected a guide who was well-acquainted with Israel — a lady whom Mother Martyria met at a gathering. When this lady learnt of my accident, she offered to take me round in her car, where I could recline, while she drove me to all the important sites and holy places in Israel for about a week. Consequently, owing to my injury, we not only acquired an excellent guide, but were able to visit places that we could never have reached without a car.

As a result of God's wonderful leadings, we came into contact with many Israelis. We met them in the streets and squares or wherever the car parked. Since our guide spoke several languages, including Hebrew, we were able to communicate with Israelis and learn of their sufferings, their hopes and their joys...

My love for this land of God and for His people grew more and more fervent. I began to understand better the great love God has for this people...I was also grateful that we could meet leading personages of the country and humble ourselves in deep contrition before them because of the crime our nation had committed against Israel.

At every encounter I was conscious of God's planning. The whole journey revolved round Israel, the people whom God loves, and the new God-given commission. Once when our car pulled up in a street in Haifa, a little boy came up to the car window. He told us cheerfully that his name was Gideon and then with childlike candour asked, 'Who are you? Where do you come from?' Suddenly he said, 'You must come to Israel and help us! We could use you.' It was a strange feeling. Was God speaking through this child to call us to His people in His land Israel? Did He have a commission there for us as Germans? We scarcely dared to mention that we came from the land that had brought such misery and horror to the Jewish people. But just as God had given this little boy an open heart for us Germans, we found the same openness in other Israelis whenever we came to them in deep grief and asked for forgiveness because of the cruel wounds that our people had inflicted upon them.

After our return home we received another call to Israel; this time not from a child, but from an influential person. 'Come to us! Help us!' God was waiting for our response as a fruit of repentance, and accordingly we sent two sisters to Israel. After studying Hebrew, they took up nursing in an Israeli hospital. Although our sisters offered their services voluntarily, accepting no salary — as a token of repentance for the crime of our nation — the fact that they were accepted as *German* sisters can only be attributed to God, to His purposes and commission.

Much as I loved Israel, I found it very hard to be parted from two of my spiritual daughters. For the first time two members of our spiritual family were to go to a far-off land, which even in those days was threatened by war. Both of them had attended the Girls' Bible Study Groups, and Mother Martyria and I had known them since their childhood. Yet I could only regard it as the grace of God and a tremendous privilege that we were finally able to send the two sisters to Israel in

March 1957. The Lord had confirmed that the Christmas wish I had made in 1954 was according to His will. A new commission had begun: to live for Israel out of repentance and love, thus fulfilling one of the desires of Jesus' heart.

When I returned from my first visit to Israel, the fire that had been kindled in me continued to blaze, and under the prompting of the Spirit I wrote a small book on Israel and later *Israel, Mein Volk (Israel, My Chosen People)*, which was then translated into several languages. I felt constrained to write these books in order to call others in our country, especially the Christians, to see our serious sin against God's chosen people. At the same time I had a burden on my heart to tell Israel about her election and God's wonderful purposes for her, His promises and the beginning of their fulfilment. The Lord granted grace and this book was well received by Christians in our country and also by Jews, some of whom rediscovered the faith of their fathers as a result.

But the fire did not die down in my heart. Love, especially when repentance is its fuel, constantly seeks new ways and means of expressing itself. Even before my journey the Holy Spirit constrained me to write a proclamation play about Israel. In the summer of 1956 in Frankfurt we performed it at the German Protestant *Kirchentag* — the first Herald Play we performed at this biannual convention. Although it bore no resemblance to modern drama, it made such an impact that people came by the thousand to see it. The spacious church was not large enough to hold the crowds of visitors, although performances were held twice daily. One night we even had to give an additional performance at 10 o'clock. Later this proclamation play about Israel was presented at other *Kirchentage* and in many cities in West Germany. As various clergymen told us, it helped to change the attitude towards Israel in churches in many parts of the country.

Thousands of guests attending our retreats over the course of the years have learnt of Israel's significance in God's plan of salvation. And those who were German have come to realize more deeply the seriousness of the crime committed by our nation. Our guests have taken part in our Prayer for Israel on Friday evenings and many have experienced a change of heart towards Israel.

But the Israel commission did not end there. In 1959 God showed me that a small branch of the sisterhood — Beth Avraham — was to be established in Jerusalem and that we were to receive the house in answer to prayer and faith. For His beloved people it would be a place where wounds would be healed and hearts would learn to trust God again. Through the ministry in Beth Avraham His people would be prepared for the coming of the Messiah. In spite of great difficulties and impossibilities, the Lord, true to His name, which is Yea and Amen, gave us this house a year later in a miraculous way.

It was all part of God's plan that the dedication of Beth Avraham took place at the same time as the opening of the Eichmann trial in 1961. All Israel was in a state of great inner turmoil as the terrible wounds of the past (1933-1945) were re-opened in public. For the first time many of Israel's young people began to comprehend the extent of our guilt as a nation; in order to spare their children, many parents had concealed the events of the past from them. At first I was deeply distressed; it seemed most unfortunate that the date of the dedication of Beth Avraham and the date of the Eichmann trial should coincide. We feared that no Israeli would attend our dedication ceremony. Who would step inside a house belonging to Germans, and Christians at that, in the present situation? Yet over a hundred Israeli guests came and the Lord in His grace used this gathering to bring some relief to their grief-stricken hearts. They could sense our love for them and that helped to melt their natural reserve and to assuage their pain.

The former mayor of Jerusalem was also present on the day of dedication, and as he gave his address, I began to understand the wisdom and love of God in allowing this festival to take place at the beginning of the Eichmann trial. He said:

Now, as this terrible trial is in process I can see the difference between this man, whose name I do not even wish to mention — especially not here — and the love I see in you. I have heard your reasons, I have also understood the cause. The source, the origin, is contrition, atonement, repentance ... The purpose is love, the means faith, trust, hope. This is what led you to open this house ...

And a Jewish author said:

> If in these days as Jews we are in danger of
> repaying hatred with hatred, you have helped
> us to overcome this temptation. There is only
> one weapon against hatred — and that is love.
> We thank you for saving us from hatred, from
> collective hatred in this hour of temptation.

How much has come as a result of that holy
hour in 1955 when the Lord linked us together
with Israel! Today our house Beth Avraham is a
place where Israelis, especially those who have
suffered in concentration camps, come for a time
of refreshment in body and soul. In addition, Beth
Avraham is a place of prayer and thus a source of
blessing.

Israel had become part of our life; her joys and
sorrows were our own. For example, when we
heard of new incidents of anti-Semitism or when
war had broken out in Israel — as in the case of
the Six Day War or the Yom Kippur War — we
felt all the more constrained to pray for God's
people. We longed to send a word of encourage-
ment to Jewish communities and the many Jews
whom we have come to know over the years both
in Israel and Germany.

The invitations to Israel were repeated. Doors
were opened and I was privileged to give lectures
in His land. Requests were made to hear 'the
unusual and incredible story of the sisterhood'.
Astonished and ashamed, I saw how Jewish
people — some elderly and sick, some who had
come from long distances — flocked to my talks,

in good weather and bad. Although the majority had only heard of the meetings by word of mouth, they came all the same. Among other things I told them about the miracles that had taken place on our little land of Canaan and they followed my lectures with keen interest and evident warmth. Their gratitude overflowed. They said that they had received fresh inspiration, that a breath of biblical life had been brought back into their biblical land and that the shattered faith of some had been restored. I felt that such responses could only come from the people God had chosen for His possession — and I had been speaking to secular audiences. For example, the day after I had held a lecture in Haifa, a newspaper review drew the following conclusion, 'The governmental departments should begin to walk the pathway of faith, trusting in the living God; then there would be an improvement in the country.'

Also in the United States and Canada, Jewish communities asked me to come and speak at their synagogues, at rabbi meetings and student meetings, and even to hold the 'sermon' during their Sabbath service. The call to repentance, arising from personal contrition and confession of guilt, reached people's hearts...

Other Literature by M. Basilea Schlink

A FORETASTE OF HEAVEN
(American edition: I FOUND THE KEY TO THE HEART
OF GOD) 416 pages, autobiography

'Since first reading this story about three years ago, I
have found it a constant companion to my devotional
reading. I turn to it for spiritual comfort and help
on many subjects such as prayer, battles of faith,
repentance, persecution, suffering, songs of praise and
thankfulness and other matters to name a few ... I
have not found a book which has taught me so much
and confirmed that God lives and works today.'

BUILDING A WALL OF PRAYER:
AN INTERCESSOR'S HANDBOOK 96 pages

When the future of a nation is in the balance, when
politics, economics and ethics fail, it is the intercessors
who can make a difference. They hold the key to
recovery, for they focus on God, from whom alone
come blessing and salvation. Everyone who knows
and loves the Lord — not just some special elite — can
be an effective intercessor. Here we are told how.

THE HOLY LAND TODAY 368 pages, 5 sketch maps

The Holy Land comes to life — a guidebook with a
difference! Pilgrims will find it an indispensable companion as they follow in the footsteps of Jesus.

JESUS BY THE SEA OF GALILEE
72 pages, 9 colour plates

'This book really appealed to me. I read it not just once,
but a second and a third time. Seldom has a book
meant so much to me. The thoughts and feelings it
evoked in me are still there, and Jesus has become real
to me in a new way.'

FOR JERUSALEM'S SAKE I WILL NOT REST 128 pages

Written after the Six Day War and in popular demand for many years now, this book is more relevant than ever. It is expressive of a deep love for the land of Israel and its people. In the reunification of Jerusalem the author sees a sign that God is working out His purpose of redemption for His people, as He promised through His prophets.

NATURE OUT OF CONTROL? 96 pages

In view of the recent floods, fires, quakes and blizzards, people are beginning to ask, 'Is God trying to tell us something?' The present age, characterized by turmoil in nature, is an opportunity to know the living God as never before. Knowing Him helps to make sense of a senseless world.

by M. Martyria Madauss

TURNING DEFEAT INTO VICTORY: DISCIPLESHIP IN THE LIGHT OF ROMANS 128 pages

Have you ever tried to get rid of a habit — and find you can't? Do you still think and do things you know are wrong, but can't stop yourself, even though you have given your life to Jesus? Do you have difficulty discerning the will of God? Then this book is for you. In simple, practical terms Mother Martyria spells out victorious Christian living on the basis of Paul's letter to the Romans. There is no such thing as a hopeless case, she concludes, since even our failures can be turned into a victory for the Lord if we move forward in faith. This is the meaning of true joy, which is dependent not on circumstances but on the assurance that God loves us as we are, but too much to leave us as we are.